PostgreSQL Administration Essentials

Discover efficient ways to administer, monitor, replicate, and handle your PostgreSQL databases

Hans-Jürgen Schönig

PUBLISHING

BIRMINGHAM - MUMBAI

PostgreSQL Administration Essentials

First published: October 2014

Production reference: 1081014

Published by Packt Publishing Ltd.
Livery Place
35 Livery Street
Birmingham B3 2PB, UK.

ISBN 978-1-78398-898-3

www.packtpub.com

Credits

Author
Hans-Jürgen Schönig

Reviewers
Debasis Roy

Sheldon E. Strauch

Steve Perkins

Vasilis Ventirozos

Commissioning Editor
Julian Ursell

Acquisition Editor
Greg Wild

Content Development Editor
Dayan Hyames

Technical Editor
Mrunmayee Patil

Copy Editors
Sayanee Mukherjee

Laxmi Subramanian

Karuna Narayanan

Project Coordinator
Harshal Ved

Proofreaders
Maria Gould

Paul Hindle

Linda Morris

Indexer
Hemangini Bari

Graphics
Sheetal Aute

Abhinash Sahu

Production Coordinators
Komal Ramchandani

Nitesh Thakur

Cover Work
Komal Ramchandani

About the Author

Hans-Jürgen Schönig and his company Cybertec Schönig & Schönig GmbH (www.postgresql-support.de) have been in professional PostgreSQL service, support, and consulting for over 15 years. He has written several books on PostgreSQL and has serviced customers around the globe. In his daily work, he focuses on performance optimization, PostgreSQL support, and training, as well as, on scalable solutions based on PostgreSQL. He likes working on complex PostgreSQL problems—especially on large-scale systems and analytical problems.

When he is not visiting customers, he is based in Wiener Neustadt, Austria.

I would like to thank my entire team here at Cybertec Schönig & Schönig GmbH (www.postgresql-support.de) for doing such a great job over the years. It is a real pleasure to work with you all here.

About the Reviewers

Debasis Roy is leading the sports team at Dhaka for Vizrt Bangladesh. He has more than 7 years of professional experience as a software engineer in Java and C++ relevant technologies. He is enthusiastic about application architecture.

He started his journey at Vizrt with a product called the Online Suite, also known as Escenic Content Engine/Studio, and is now continuing with products related to Viz Sports. Vizrt provides real-time 3D graphics, studio automation, sports analysis, and asset management tools for the broadcast industry—interactive and virtual solutions, animations, maps, weather forecasts, video editing, and compositing tools.

He has also reviewed the book *RESTful Java Web Services Security*, *Packt Publishing*.

> I would like to thank Packt Publishing for giving me the opportunity to review this wonderful book and for helping me learn new things.

Sheldon E. Strauch is a 20-year veteran of software consulting at companies such as IBM, Sears, Ernst & Young, and Kraft Foods. He has a Bachelor's degree in Business Administration and leverages his technical skills to improve the business' self-awareness. His interests include data gathering, management, and mining; maps and mapping; business intelligence; and application of data analysis for continuous improvement. He is currently focused on development of an end-to-end data management and mining at Enova International, a financial services company located in Chicago. In his spare time, he enjoys the performing arts, particularly music, and traveling with his wife, Marilyn.

Steve Perkins is the author of the book *Hibernate Search by Example*, *Packt Publishing*, and has over 15 years of experience working with enterprise Java. He lives in Atlanta, GA, USA with his wife, Amanda, and their son, Andrew. He currently works as an Architect at BetterCloud, where he writes software for the Google Cloud Platform.

When he is not writing code, he plays fiddle and guitar, and enjoys working with music production software. You can visit his technical blog at `http://steveperkins.net/` and follow him on Twitter at `@stevedperkins`.

Vasilis Ventirozos has been working with databases for more than a decade on mission-critical applications for companies in both the telcos and lottery industries. While he has worked with a number of database technologies, he considers Postgres as his database of choice. He currently works at OmniTI, a full stack IT services company, focused on highly-scalable web infrastructure, providing PostgreSQL-related consulting and management.

www.PacktPub.com

Support files, eBooks, discount offers, and more

You might want to visit www.PacktPub.com for support files and downloads related to your book.

Did you know that Packt offers eBook versions of every book published, with PDF and ePub files available? You can upgrade to the eBook version at www.PacktPub.com and as a print book customer, you are entitled to a discount on the eBook copy. Get in touch with us at service@packtpub.com for more details.

At www.PacktPub.com, you can also read a collection of free technical articles, sign up for a range of free newsletters and receive exclusive discounts and offers on Packt books and eBooks.

http://PacktLib.PacktPub.com

Do you need instant solutions to your IT questions? PacktLib is Packt's online digital book library. Here, you can access, read and search across Packt's entire library of books.

Why subscribe?

- Fully searchable across every book published by Packt
- Copy and paste, print and bookmark content
- On demand and accessible via web browser

Free access for Packt account holders

If you have an account with Packt at www.PacktPub.com, you can use this to access PacktLib today and view nine entirely free books. Simply use your login credentials for immediate access.

Table of Contents

Preface   1

Chapter 1: Installing PostgreSQL   5

  Preparing your setup   5

    Understanding the PostgreSQL version numbers   6

     Choosing the right version   6

    Installing binary packages   6

     Installing PostgreSQL on Debian or Ubuntu   7

     Installing PostgreSQL on Red-Hat-based systems   8

    Compiling PostgreSQL from source   8

     How it works   9

     Installing the contrib packages   10

     Finalizing your installation   11

     Creating a database instance   11

     Firing up PostgreSQL   12

  Understanding the existing databases   13

  Creating databases   14

  Summary   15

Chapter 2: Indexing and Performance Tuning   17

  Using simple binary trees   17

    Preparing the data   18

  Understanding the concept of execution plans   19

    Calculating costs   20

    Drawing important conclusions   21

    Creating indexes   22

    Analyzing the performance of a query   23

    The internal structure of a B-tree index   24

     Understanding the B-tree internals   25

     Providing a sorted order   25

    Combined indexes   26

    Partial indexes   28

Dealing with different types of indexes   **29**
Detecting missing indexes   **29**
Detecting slow queries   **32**
How to reset statistics   34
Adjusting memory parameters   **35**
Optimizing shared buffers   35
Considering huge pages   36
Tweaking work_mem   37
Improving maintenance_work_mem   41
Adjusting effective_cache_size   41
Summary   **41**

Chapter 3: Users and Permissions   **43**
Understanding PostgreSQL security   **43**
Configuring the TCP   44
Managing network authentication   45
Managing contradictions   46
Authentication methods available   47
Some more examples   48
Handling SSL   49
Changing pg_hba.conf   50
Handling instance-level permissions   51
Creating roles   51
Modifying and dropping roles   54
Controlling database-level permissions   56
Understanding schema-level permissions   57
Handling table-level permissions   59
Managing column rights   61
Improving security with SELinux   61
Summary   **63**

Chapter 4: Managing Logfiles   **65**
Understanding the PostgreSQL log architecture   **65**
Configuring log destinations   66
Creating local logfiles   66
Using syslog   67
Configuring logs on Windows   68
Performance considerations   68
Configuring the amount of log output   **69**
Making logs more readable   70
Additional settings   71
Making log creation more fine grained   **72**
Logging selectively   72
Focusing on slow queries   73

Silencing notices   73
Summary   **74**
Chapter 5: Backup and Recovery   **75**
  Importing and exporting data   **75**
    Using the COPY command   75
      Basic operations of the COPY command   76
      Making use of pipes   78
  Performing backups   **79**
    Handling pg_dump   79
      More sophisticated dumping   79
      Performing partial replays   80
      Passing users and passwords   81
    Dumping an entire instance   82
      Understanding backups and user creation   83
  Summary   **84**
Chapter 6: Handling Replication and Improving Performance   **85**
  Understanding the PostgreSQL transaction log   **85**
    The purpose of the transaction log   86
    Inspecting the size of the transaction log   87
  Configuring the checkpoints   **88**
    Optimizing the checkpoints   89
      Configuring the distance between checkpoints   89
      Controlling writes   90
  Setting up an asynchronous replication   **92**
    Obtaining a high-level overview   92
    Setting up replication step by step   93
      Preparing the slave   93
      Configuring the master   93
      Fetching an initial backup   94
      Creating and modifying the recovery.conf file   96
      Firing up the slave   96
      Turning slaves into masters   97
  Upgrading to synchronous replication   **98**
  Improving and monitoring the replication   **99**
    Keeping an eye on streaming   99
    Making things more robust   100
    Managing conflicts   101
  Handling point-in-time recovery   **103**
    Setting up PITR   103
    Replaying transaction logs   105
  Understanding timelines   **106**
    The importance of timelines   108
  Summary   **108**

Chapter 7: Monitoring PostgreSQL   **109**

Understanding the system statistics of PostgreSQL   **109**

Checking out the pg_stat_activity file   110
Monitoring databases   111
Monitoring tables   113
Monitoring indexes   114
Checking out the information in the background writer   115
Resetting statistics   116

Integrating Nagios   **117**
Handling Linux cgroups   **118**

Setting up cgroups   118

Summary   **120**

Index   **121**

Preface

PostgreSQL Administration Essentials... that sounds interesting! I think these were the first things I had in my mind when I was confronted with the idea of writing one more book on PostgreSQL. And, voila, here I am writing those first lines of this new book on PostgreSQL. My hope is that this little book will serve you well—providing help whenever it is needed.

Since I started my career as a PostgreSQL consultant (`www.postgresql-support.de`), there has always been a demand for a short, compact book on PostgreSQL administration. No big bloated thing but a book dealing exclusively with what people really need in their daily life. A small thing people can have on their tables all the time and which can be used for everyday administration problems. I am glad that I got the chance to take a shot on a book like that.

What this book covers

Chapter 1, Installing PostgreSQL, introduces you to the installation process and helps in learning how to install binaries, as well as, to compile PostgreSQL from source.

Chapter 2, Indexing and Performance Tuning, introduces you to indexes. This chapter is entirely dedicated to indexes, as well as, to performance-related issues. Indexes are a corner stone when it comes to performance and; therefore, a lot of focus is on indexes.

Chapter 3, Users and Permissions, introduces you to the security system. The basic concepts of the PostgreSQL security system, as well as, some advanced concepts are outlined in this chapter.

Chapter 4, Managing Logfiles, covers the managing of logfiles.

Chapter 5, Backup and Recovery, outlines how textual backups can be created and restored, as saving and restoring data is an essential task of every system administrator.

Chapter 6, Handling Replication and Improving Performance, covers various flavors of replication, as well as, PITR. Synchronous, as well as, asynchronous replications are also covered in this chapter.

Chapter 7, Monitoring PostgreSQL, covers monitoring to make sure that your systems are available and productive. To make sure that PostgreSQL stays up and running, monitoring is an important topic.

What you need for this book

The entire book has been written on a Linux system, as well as, on Mac OS X. Some parts are Unix-specific. However, the biggest part of the book will also work just fine with Microsoft Windows.

So, all you will need is Windows or some Unix system to follow the given examples outlining all the technical issues subjected to this book.

Who this book is for

This book has been written for those who want to administer a PostgreSQL database fast and efficiently. It contains valuable information to make your life as easy as possible. During your daily work, this little book will help you to quickly detect problems, as well as bottlenecks.

Conventions

In this book, you will find a number of styles of text that distinguish between different kinds of information. Here are some examples of these styles, and an explanation of their meaning.

Code words in text, database table names, folder names, filenames, file extensions, pathnames, dummy URLs, user input, and Twitter handles are shown as follows: "Note that we use -1 here for simplicity reasons."

Any command-line input or output is written as follows:

```
pg_ctl -D /data -l /dev/null start
```

New terms and important words are shown in bold.

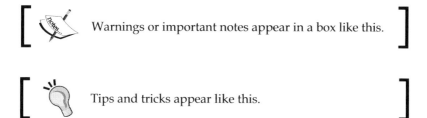

[Warnings or important notes appear in a box like this.]

[Tips and tricks appear like this.]

Reader feedback

Feedback from our readers is always welcome. Let us know what you think about this book—what you liked or may have disliked. Reader feedback is important for us to develop titles that you really get the most out of.

To send us general feedback, simply send an e-mail to feedback@packtpub.com, and mention the book title via the subject of your message.

If there is a topic that you have expertise in and you are interested in either writing or contributing to a book, see our author guide on www.packtpub.com/authors.

Customer support

Now that you are the proud owner of a Packt book, we have a number of things to help you to get the most from your purchase.

Errata

Although we have taken every care to ensure the accuracy of our content, mistakes do happen. If you find a mistake in one of our books—maybe a mistake in the text or the code—we would be grateful if you would report this to us. By doing so, you can save other readers from frustration and help us improve subsequent versions of this book. If you find any errata, please report them by visiting http://www.packtpub. com/submit-errata, selecting your book, clicking on the **errata submission form** link, and entering the details of your errata. Once your errata are verified, your submission will be accepted and the errata will be uploaded on our website, or added to any list of existing errata, under the Errata section of that title. Any existing errata can be viewed by selecting your title from http://www.packtpub.com/support.

Piracy

Piracy of copyright material on the Internet is an ongoing problem across all media. At Packt, we take the protection of our copyright and licenses very seriously. If you come across any illegal copies of our works, in any form on the Internet, please provide us with the location address or website name immediately so that we can pursue a remedy.

Please contact us at copyright@packtpub.com with a link to the suspected pirated material.

We appreciate your help in protecting our authors, and our ability to bring you valuable content.

Questions

You can contact us at questions@packtpub.com if you are having a problem with any aspect of the book, and we will do our best to address it.

Installing PostgreSQL

1

In this chapter, we will cover the installation process of PostgreSQL. You will learn how to install binary packages and see how PostgreSQL can be compiled from source. Compiling from source is especially important if you happen to be using platforms on which no binaries are available (for example, AIX, HPUX, and so on).

We will cover the following topics in this chapter:

- Preparing your setup
- Installing binary packages
- Compiling PostgreSQL from source
- Understanding the existing databases
- Creating databases

You will see how easy it is to make PostgreSQL work in a couple of minutes.

Preparing your setup

Before we dig into the actual installation process and see how things can be put to work, it makes sense to talk a little bit about the PostgreSQL version numbers. Understanding the PostgreSQL versioning policy will give you valuable insights, especially with respect to your upgrade policy, downtime management, and so on.

Understanding the PostgreSQL version numbers

As you might have already seen, a PostgreSQL version number consists of three digits. The logic of the version number is as follows:

- **Minor releases**: 9.4.2, 9.4.1, 9.4.1
- **Major releases**: 9.4.0, 9.3.0, 9.2.0
- **N.0.0 releases (super major)**: 9.0.0, 8.0.0, 7.0.0

The distinction between the preceding three types of releases is pretty important. Why is that? Well, if you happen to upgrade to a new minor release (say, from 9.4.1 to 9.4.3), all you have to do is stop the database and start the new binaries. There is no need to touch the data. In short, the amount of downtime needed is basically close to zero.

Note that a minor release only contains bug fixes, improvements in the documentation, and so on. It will never add new features, change the functionality, or remove existing stuff.

 You can safely update to a more recent minor release to improve reliability. The risk involved is negligible.

In case of a major version change, you definitely have to plan things a little better because updates are a bit more complicated (`pg_dump` / `pg_restore` or `pg_upgrade`).

Choosing the right version

When I am training people, they ask me on a regular basis which version of PostgreSQL they should use. The answer to this question is simple; if you have the ability to decide freely, it is absolutely safe to use the latest stable release of PostgreSQL, even if it is a "zero" release (which is equal to 9.4.0, 9.3.0, and so on).

Installing binary packages

After this little introduction to PostgreSQL versioning, we can move forward and see how binary packages can be installed. Nowadays, most people use binary packages that are shipped with their preferred Linux distribution. These packages are tested, easy to use, and readily available.

In this chapter, we will show you how to install PostgreSQL on Debian or Ubuntu and on Red-Hat-based systems.

Installing PostgreSQL on Debian or Ubuntu

Let's focus on installing PostgreSQL on Debian or Ubuntu first. The key point here is that it is recommended to add the PostgreSQL repositories to Ubuntu. The reason is that many Linux distributions, including Ubuntu, ship very old and outdated versions of PostgreSQL in their standard setup. If you don't want to miss a couple of years of PostgreSQL development, adding the current repositories will be highly beneficial to you. The process of adding the repositories is as follows:

1. Create a file called `/etc/apt/sources.list.d/pgdg.list`, and add a line for the PostgreSQL repository (the following steps can be done as a root user or by using `sudo`). Alternatively, `/etc/apt/sources.list` is a place to put the line:

   ```
   deb http://apt.postgresql.org/pub/repos/apt/ YOUR_DEBIAN_VERSION_
   HERE-pgdg main
   ```

2. So, in case of Wheezy, the following line will be useful:

   ```
   deb http://apt.postgresql.org/pub/repos/apt/ wheezy-pgdg main
   ```

3. Once we add the repository, we can import the signing key:

   ```
   $# wget --quiet -O - \
     https://www.postgresql.org/media/keys/ACCC4CF8.asc | \
     apt-key add -
   OK
   ```

4. Once the key has been added, we can update our package information and install PostgreSQL:

   ```
   apt-get update
   ```

5. In our case, we will install PostgreSQL 9.4. Of course, you can also decide to use 9.3 or any other recent version you desire:

   ```
   apt-get install "postgresql-9.4"
   ```

6. All relevant packages will be downloaded automatically, and the system will instantly fire up PostgreSQL.

7. Once all these steps have been performed, you are ready for action. You can try to connect to the database:

   ```
   root@chantal:~# su - postgres
   $ psql postgres
   psql (9.4.1)
   Type "help" for help.
   postgres=#
   ```

Installing PostgreSQL on Red-Hat-based systems

The installation process on Red Hat-based distributions works in a pretty similar way. Many distributions use RPM packages. The following URL shows the distributions for which we are currently ready to use RPMs: `http://yum.postgresql.org/repopackages.php`.

The first thing to do is to install an RPM package containing all the repository information. Once this is done, we can easily fetch PostgreSQL RPMs from the repository and fire things up in almost no time.

In our example, we chose **Fedora 20** as our distribution. To enable the repository, we can run the following command (as root):

```
yum install http://yum.postgresql.org/9.4/fedora/fedora-20-x86_64/pgdg-fedora94-9.4-1.noarch.rpm
```

Once the repository has been added, we can install PostgreSQL by using the following commands:

```
yum install postgresql94-server postgresql94-contrib
/usr/pgsql-9.4/bin/postgresql94-setup initdb
systemctl enable postgresql-9.4.service
systemctl start postgresql-9.4.service
```

The first command (`yum install`) will fetch the packages from the repository and install them on your server. Once this is done, we can prepare a database instance and initialize it.

Finally, we enable the service and start it up. Our database server is now ready for action.

Compiling PostgreSQL from source

So far, you've seen how to install binary packages. However, in some cases, you might want to compile PostgreSQL from source all by yourself. There are several reasons for this:

- **SLAs**: You might have to provide an old version, which is not available as package anymore, to fulfill some SLA agreements.

- **No packages available**: On your favorite flavor of Linux, there is most likely a package containing PostgreSQL available always. However, what about AIX, Solaris, HPUX, and others?

- **Custom patches**: Some people write custom patches to enhance PostgreSQL.

- **Split directories**: You might want to split the binary and library directories and make sure that PostgreSQL does not integrate tightly into the existing OS.

- **Configure options**: Custom configure options, or some other options, to enable `dtrace`.

How it works

Before we get started, we have to download the tarball from `http://ftp.postgresql.org/pub/source/`. There, you will find one directory per version of PostgreSQL. In our case, we have downloaded PostgreSQL 9.4.1, and we will use it throughout this chapter.

The first thing we have to do is to extract the tar archive:

```
tar xvfz postgresql-9.4.1.tar.gz
```

This will create a directory containing the PostgreSQL source code. Once we have entered this directory, we can call `configure`, which will then check your system to see if all libraries you need are present. It generates vital parts of the build infrastructure.

Here is how it works:

```
./configure --prefix=/usr/local/pg941
```

In our example, we used the most simplistic of all configurations. We want to install the binaries to a directory called `/usr/local/pg941`. Note that this is not where the data will end up; it is where the executables will reside. If you don't define `-prefix`, the default installation path will be `/usr/local/pgsql`.

Of course, there is a lot more. Try running the following command:

```
./configure --help
```

If you run the preceding command, you will see that there are some more features that can be turned on (for example, `--with-perl` or `--with-python`) in case you are planning to write stored procedures in Perl or Python.

In some cases, you might find that our operating system lacks libraries needed to compile PostgreSQL properly. Some of the most common candidates are `libreadline-dev` and `zlib-dev` (of course there are some more). These two libraries are needed to enable the command-line history as well as to give support for compression. We highly recommend providing both libraries to PostgreSQL.

Keep in mind that the two previously defined libraries have slightly different names on different Linux distributions because every Linux distribution uses slightly different naming conventions.

If you are compiling on a more exotic Unix operating system such as Solaris, AIX, and so on, we recommend you to check out the documentation regarding the platform specifications.

We can move forward and actually compile PostgreSQL, using the following commands:

```
make
make install
```

You just have to call `make` and `make install` (as root) and wait for a few seconds. In this case, we simply use one CPU core to build PostgreSQL. If you want to scale out the build process to many CPU cores, you can use `-j`, shown as follows:

```
make -j 8
```

The `-j 8` command will tell `make` to do up to `8` things in parallel, if possible. Adding parallelism to the build process will definitely speed up the process. It is not uncommon to build PostgreSQL in 30 seconds or less if there are enough CPU cores on board.

Installing the contrib packages

It is highly recommended to install the PostgreSQL `contrib` packages as well. **Contrib** is a set of additional modules that can be used for different purposes such as creating database links from PostgreSQL, to PostgreSQL, or for adding an additional indexing functionality.

If you are installing PostgreSQL from binary packages, you can simply install one more package (for example, `postgresql-9.3-contrib`). If you happen to install from source, you have to perform the following steps:

```
cd contrib
make
make install
```

Of course, you can also use the `-j` flag again to scale out to more than just one CPU. The `make install` command will need root permissions again (for example, via `sudo`).

Finalizing your installation

Once the binaries have been installed, we can move forward and finalize our installation. The following steps are to be carried out in order to finalize our installation:

- Creating and configuring a user to run PostgreSQL
- Creating a database instance
- Deploying the `init` scripts

If you have installed PostgreSQL from binary packages, the system will automatically create a user for PostgreSQL. If you happen to compile it yourself, you have to create the operating system user yourself too.

Depending on the operating system you are using, this works in a slightly different way. On Ubuntu, for instance, you can call `adduser` on Red Hat and `useradd` on CentOS. I really recommend looking up the procedure to create a user in your operating system manual.

In general, it's best practice to create a user named `postgres`; however, a nonroot user will also do. I just recommend sticking to the standard to make life easier on the administration front.

Once the user has been created, it is, in general, a good idea to prepare your infrastructure for PostgreSQL. This implies adjusting your `$PATH` environment variable. On most Linux systems, this can be done in your `.bash_profile` or `.bashrc` file. Having your favorite PostgreSQL tools in your path will make life simple and a lot easier.

Finally, we can add the `init` scripts to the system. In `postgresql-9.4.1/contrib/start-scripts`, you will find `init` scripts for Linux, Mac OS X, and FreeBSD. These scripts are a good framework to make your `init` process work as expected.

Creating a database instance

Once we compile PostgreSQL and prepare ourselves to launch PostgreSQL, we can create a so-called PostgreSQL database instance. What is a database instance? Well, whenever you start PostgreSQL, you are actually firing up a database instance. So, the instance is really a central thing; it is that which contains all the databases, users, tablespaces, and so on.

In PostgreSQL, a database instance always resides in a database directory. In our example, we want to create the instance under /data:

```
mkdir /data
chown postgres.postgres /data
su - postgres
initdb -D /data -E unicode
```

First, we created the directory and assigned it to the postgres user. Then, we created the database instance. The important part here is that we explicitly stated (-E unicode) that we want UTF-8 to be the default character set in our system. If we don't explicitly tell the system what to use, it will check out the locale settings and use the Unix locale as the default for the instance. This might not be the desired configuration for your setup, so it is better to explicitly define the character set.

Also, instead of using -D here, we can set $PGDATA to tell PostgreSQL where the desired place for the database instance is going to be. There's also an initdb --help command that will reveal a handful of additional configuration options.

At this point, we won't go into all the configuration options as it is out of the scope of this book. However, we will point out some really useful flags, described as follows:

- -A: This defines the default authentication method of local connections. Many people use trust, md5, or peer for this option.
- -E and --locale: This defines your desired character set and locale settings.
- -k: This setting will require PostgreSQL to create data page checksums. It is highly recommended to use this setting for mission critical data. The overhead of the page checksums is virtually zero, so you will get a lot more protection for your data at virtually no cost.

Once we create our database instance, we can start our database server.

Firing up PostgreSQL

Firing up PostgreSQL is easy. If we used binary packages, we can use the /etc/init.d/postgresql start or service postgresql start command (as root or by using sudo).

Note that on some Linux distros, it might be necessary to add a version number to the service (for example, /etc/init.d/postgresql-9.4 start). On non-Linux systems, you have to check out your corresponding init routines.

In case you have not installed the `start` scripts, you can fire up PostgreSQL manually. Assuming that our database instance resides in `/data`, it works like this:

```
pg_ctl -D /data -l /dev/null start
```

In the preceding command, `pg_ctl` is the tool to control PostgreSQL, `-D` tells the system where to find the database instance, `-l /dev/null` tells our database server to send the log information to `/dev/null`, and `start` will simply make the instance fire up.

Note that we use `-l` here for simplicity reasons. In later chapters, you will learn how to set up proper logging using the PostgreSQL onboard infrastructure.

Installing PostgreSQL is as simple as that.

Understanding the existing databases

Once the database has been launched, we can connect to PostgreSQL using a `psql` frontend:

```
psql postgres
```

Ideally, you connect to a database called `postgres`, which can be found in any database instance. Some systems don't encourage people to log in as a `postgres` user. Therefore, you might want to use `sudo` here as well to log in to PostgreSQL. If this works for you, you can make PostgreSQL display a list of existing databases, where `\l` will do the job:

```
postgres=# \x
Expanded display is on.
postgres=# \l
List of databases
-[ RECORD 1 ]-----+---------------------
Name              | postgres
Owner             | postgres
Encoding          | UTF8
Collate           | en_US.UTF-8
Ctype             | en_US.UTF-8
Access privileges |
-[ RECORD 2 ]-----+---------------------
Name              | template0
Owner             | postgres
```

```
Encoding           | UTF8
Collate            | en_US.UTF-8
Ctype              | en_US.UTF-8
Access privileges  | =c/postgres
                   | postgres=CTc/postgres
-[ RECORD 3 ]-----+---------------------
Name               | template1
Owner              | postgres
Encoding           | UTF8
Collate            | en_US.UTF-8
Ctype              | en_US.UTF-8
Access privileges  | =c/postgres
                   | postgres=CTc/postgres
```

Congratulations, you've completed your first task using the `psql` shell. If you executed \l as proposed, you might have seen that the table is too wide to be displayed properly. To avoid this, you can use \x to transpose the output and display each column as a separate line. This little feature can come in handy whenever you have to read a wide table.

> If you want to customize the `psql` shell for your needs, you might want to consider writing a `.psqlrc` file. It can automatically set things such as \x for you on every login.

In an empty database instance, you will already find the three existing databases `template0`, `template1`, and `postgres`. The rule for you as an end user is simple: always connect to the `postgres` database and try to avoid connections to the `template` databases (`template0` does not allow connections anyway); these databases are only here to act as a role model in case you create a new database. Make sure that no useless objects are in `template0` or `template1` because whenever you create an additional database, these useless objects are cloned.

Creating databases

The next logical step is to create a new database. For this operation, PostgreSQL provides an instruction called CREATE DATABASE. Here is the syntax of this vital command:

```
postgres=# \h CREATE DATABASE
Command:    CREATE DATABASE
```

```
Description: create a new database
Syntax:
CREATE DATABASE name
    [ [ WITH ] [ OWNER [=] user_name ]
           [ TEMPLATE [=] template ]
           [ ENCODING [=] encoding ]
           [ LC_COLLATE [=] lc_collate ]
           [ LC_CTYPE [=] lc_ctype ]
           [ TABLESPACE [=] tablespace_name ]
           [ CONNECTION LIMIT [=] connlimit ] ] ]
```

The \h command is very convenient to use; it provides you with the syntax of basically every command in the system. In short, \h makes life really easy.

In our case, we can see which options CREATE DATABASE provides. First, we can define the name of the newly created database. The TEMPLATE parameter can be used to physically clone an existing database (if you don't use this one, template1 will be cloned by default). The ENCODING and LC_* parameters are needed in case you want to use encodings and locales different from the default one. Finally, we can make use of a tablespace (which will be dealt with later on in this book), and PostgreSQL provides a way to limit the number of concurrent connections to the database.

In our example, we create a simple database:

```
postgres=# CREATE DATABASE test;
CREATE DATABASE
```

If this succeeds, we are ready to connect to our newly created database. We can even do so without psql:

```
postgres=# \c test
psql (9.4.1, server 9.4.1)
You are now connected to database "test" as user "postgres".
```

Summary

In this chapter, you learned how to install PostgreSQL binary packages and compile PostgreSQL from source. You also learned how to create database instances and create simple databases inside your instance.

The next chapter will be dedicated to some of the biggest problems in the database world. You will be guided through indexing and detecting performance bottlenecks.

2
Indexing and Performance Tuning

You might wonder why a book about PostgreSQL administration actually contains a chapter on indexing and performance tuning. The answer is quite simple actually; extensive experience in database engineering and support shows that a poor indexing strategy will, on a regular basis, totally cripple user experience as well as performance. It happens on a regular basis that a bad overall indexing strategy totally destroys user experience as well as performance.

Therefore, it is one of my primary goals to provide as much information as possible about hunting down wrong or missing indexes so that you, the reader, can easily optimize your system to enjoy the full power of PostgreSQL.

In this chapter, you will be guided through PostgreSQL indexing, and you will learn how to fix performance issues and find performance bottlenecks. Understanding indexing will be vital to your success as a DBA — you cannot count on software engineers to get this right straightaway. It will be you, the DBA, who will face problems caused by bad indexing in the field. For the sake of your beloved sleep at night, this chapter is about PostgreSQL indexing.

Using simple binary trees

In this section, you will learn about simple binary trees and how the PostgreSQL optimizer treats the trees. Once you understand the basic decisions taken by the optimizer, you can move on to more complex index types.

Preparing the data

Indexing does not change user experience too much, unless you have a reasonable amount of data in your database—the more data you have, the more indexing can help to boost things. Therefore, we have to create some simple sets of data to get us started. Here is a simple way to populate a table:

```
test=# CREATE TABLE t_test (id serial, name text);
CREATE TABLE
test=# INSERT INTO t_test (name) SELECT 'hans' FROM
  generate_series(1, 2000000);
INSERT 0 2000000
test=# INSERT INTO t_test (name) SELECT 'paul' FROM
  generate_series(1, 2000000);
INSERT 0 2000000
```

In our example, we created a table consisting of two columns. The first column is simply an automatically created integer value. The second column contains the name.

Once the table is created, we start to populate it. It's nice and easy to generate a set of numbers using the generate_series function. In our example, we simply generate two million numbers. Note that these numbers will not be put into the table; we will still fetch the numbers from the sequence using generate_series to create two million hans and rows featuring paul, shown as follows:

```
test=# SELECT * FROM t_test LIMIT 3;
 id | name
----+------
  1 | hans
  2 | hans
  3 | hans
(3 rows)
```

Once we create a sufficient amount of data, we can run a simple test. The goal is to simply count the rows we have inserted. The main issue here is: how can we find out how long it takes to execute this type of query? The \timing command will do the job for you:

```
test=# \timing
Timing is on.
```

As you can see, \timing will add the total runtime to the result. This makes it quite easy for you to see if a query turns out to be a problem or not:

```
test=# SELECT count(*) FROM t_test;
  count
---------
 4000000
(1 row)
Time: 316.628 ms
```

As you can see in the preceding code, the time required is approximately 300 milliseconds. This might not sound like a lot, but it actually is. 300 ms means that we can roughly execute three queries per CPU per second. On an 8-Core box, this would translate to roughly 25 queries per second. For many applications, this will be enough; but do you really want to buy an 8-Core box to handle just 25 concurrent users, and do you want your entire box to work just on this simple query? Probably not!

Understanding the concept of execution plans

It is impossible to understand the use of indexes without understanding the concept of execution plans. Whenever you execute a query in PostgreSQL, it generally goes through four central steps, described as follows:

- **Parser**: PostgreSQL will check the syntax of the statement.
- **Rewrite system**: PostgreSQL will rewrite the query (for example, rules and views are handled by the rewrite system).
- **Optimizer** or **planner**: PostgreSQL will come up with a smart plan to execute the query as efficiently as possible. At this step, the system will decide whether or not to use indexes.
- **Executor**: Finally, the execution plan is taken by the executor and the result is generated.

Being able to understand and read execution plans is an essential task of every DBA. To extract the plan from the system, all you need to do is use the explain command, shown as follows:

```
test=# explain SELECT count(*) FROM t_test;
                           QUERY PLAN
--------------------------------------------------------
```

```
Aggregate  (cost=71622.00..71622.01 rows=1 width=0)
   ->  Seq Scan on t_test  (cost=0.00..61622.00
                          rows=4000000 width=0)
(2 rows)

Time: 0.370 ms
```

In our case, it took us less than a millisecond to calculate the execution plan. Once you have the plan, you can read it from right to left. In our case, PostgreSQL will perform a sequential scan and aggregate the data returned by the sequential scan. It is important to mention that each step is assigned to a certain number of costs. The total cost for the sequential scan is 61,622 penalty points (more details about penalty points will be outlined a little later). The overall cost of the query is 71,622.01. What are costs?

Well, costs are just an arbitrary number calculated by the system based on some rules. The higher the costs, the slower a query is expected to be. Always keep in mind that these costs are just a way for PostgreSQL to estimate things—they are in no way a reliable number related to anything in the real world (such as time or amount of I/O needed).

In addition to the costs, PostgreSQL estimates that the sequential scan will yield around four million rows. It also expects the aggregation to return just a single row. These two estimates happen to be precise, but it is not always so.

Calculating costs

When in training, people often ask how PostgreSQL does its cost calculations. Consider a simple example like the one we have next. It works in a pretty simple way. Generally, there are two types of costs: I/O costs and CPU costs.

To come up with I/O costs, we have to figure out the size of the table we are dealing with first:

```
test=# SELECT pg_relation_size('t_test'),
  pg_size_pretty(pg_relation_size('t_test'));
 pg_relation_size | pg_size_pretty
------------------+----------------
        177127424 | 169 MB
(1 row)
```

The pg_relation_size command is a fast way to see how large a table is. Of course, reading a large number (many digits) is somewhat hard, so it is possible to fetch the size of the table in a much prettier format. In our example, the size is roughly 170 MB.

Let's move on now. In PostgreSQL, a table consists of 8,000 blocks. If we divide the size of the table by 8,192 bytes, we will end up with exactly 21,622 blocks. This is how PostgreSQL estimates I/O costs of a sequential scan. If a table is read completely, each block will receive exactly one penalty point, or any number defined by `seq_page_cost`:

```
test=# SHOW seq_page_cost;
 seq_page_cost
---------------
 1
(1 row)
```

To count this number, we have to send four million rows through the CPU (`cpu_tuple_cost`), and we also have to count these 4 million rows (`cpu_operator_cost`). So, the calculation looks like this:

- For the sequential scan: *21622*1 + 4000000*0.01 (cpu_tuple_cost) = 61622*
- For the aggregation: *61622 + 4000000*0.0025 (cpu_operator_cost) = 71622*

This is exactly the number that we see in the plan.

Drawing important conclusions

Of course, you will never do this by hand. However, there are some important conclusions to be drawn:

- The cost model in PostgreSQL is a simplification of the real world
- The costs can hardly be translated to real execution times
- The cost of reading from a slow disk is the same as the cost of reading from a fast disk
- It is hard to take caching into account

If the optimizer comes up with a bad plan, it is possible to adapt the costs either globally in `postgresql.conf`, or by changing the session variables, shown as follows:

```
test=# SET seq_page_cost TO 10;
SET
```

This statement inflated the costs at will. It can be a handy way to fix the missed estimates, leading to bad performance and, therefore, to poor execution times.

This is what the query plan will look like using the inflated costs:

```
test=# explain SELECT count(*) FROM t_test;
                     QUERY PLAN
-------------------------------------------------------
 Aggregate  (cost=266220.00..266220.01 rows=1 width=0)
   ->  Seq Scan on t_test  (cost=0.00..256220.00
          rows=4000000 width=0)
(2 rows)
```

It is important to understand the PostgreSQL code model in detail because many people have completely wrong ideas about what is going on inside the PostgreSQL optimizer. Offering a basic explanation will hopefully shed some light on this important topic and allow administrators a deeper understanding of the system.

Creating indexes

After this introduction, we can deploy our first index. As we stated before, runtimes of several hundred milliseconds for simple queries are not acceptable. To fight these unusually high execution times, we can turn to CREATE INDEX, shown as follows:

```
test=# \h CREATE INDEX
Command:     CREATE INDEX
Description: define a new index
Syntax:
CREATE [ UNIQUE ] INDEX [ CONCURRENTLY ] [ name ]
  ON table_name [ USING method ]
    ( { column_name | ( expression ) }
   [ COLLATE collation ] [ opclass ]
   [ ASC | DESC ] [ NULLS { FIRST | LAST } ]
    [, ...] )
     [ WITH ( storage_parameter = value [, ... ] ) ]
     [ TABLESPACE tablespace_name ]
     [ WHERE predicate ]
```

In the most simplistic case, we can create a normal B-tree index on the ID column and see what happens:

```
test=# CREATE INDEX idx_id ON t_test (id);
CREATE INDEX
Time: 3996.909 ms
```

B-tree indexes are the default index structure in PostgreSQL. Internally, they are also called **B+ tree**, as described by Lehman-Yao.

On this box (AMD, 4 Ghz), we can build the B-tree index in around 4 seconds, without any database side tweaks. Once the index is in place, the SELECT command will be executed at lightning speed:

```
test=# SELECT * FROM t_test WHERE id = 423423;
   id   | name
--------+------
 423423 | hans
(1 row)
Time: 0.384 ms
```

The query executes in less than a millisecond. Keep in mind that this already includes displaying the data, and the query is a lot faster internally.

Analyzing the performance of a query

How do we know that the query is actually a lot faster? In the previous section, you saw EXPLAIN in action already. However, there is a little more to know about this command.

You can add some instructions to EXPLAIN to make it a lot more verbose, as shown here:

```
test=# \h EXPLAIN
Command:     EXPLAIN
Description: show the execution plan of a statement
Syntax:
EXPLAIN [ ( option [, ...] ) ] statement
EXPLAIN [ ANALYZE ] [ VERBOSE ] statement
```

In the preceding code, the term option can be one of the following:

```
ANALYZE [ boolean ]
VERBOSE [ boolean ]
COSTS [ boolean ]
BUFFERS [ boolean ]
TIMING [ boolean ]
FORMAT { TEXT | XML | JSON | YAML }
```

Consider the following example:

```
test=# EXPLAIN (ANALYZE TRUE, VERBOSE true, COSTS TRUE,
   TIMING true) SELECT * FROM t_test WHERE id = 423423;
                    QUERY PLAN
-------------------------------------------------------
 Index Scan using idx_id on public.t_test
   (cost=0.43..8.45 rows=1 width=9)
   (actual time=0.016..0.018 rows=1 loops=1)
    Output: id, name
    Index Cond: (t_test.id = 423423)
 Total runtime: 0.042 ms
(4 rows)

Time: 0.536 ms
```

The ANALYZE function does a special form of execution. It is a good way to figure out which part of the query burned most of the time. Again, we can read things inside out. In addition to the estimated costs of the query, we can also see the real execution time. In our case, the index scan takes 0.018 milliseconds. Fast, isn't it? Given these timings, you can see that displaying the result actually takes a huge fraction of the time.

The beauty of EXPLAIN ANALYZE is that it shows costs and execution times for every step of the process. This is important for you to familiarize yourself with this kind of output because when a programmer hits your desk complaining about bad performance, it is necessary to dig into this kind of stuff quickly. In many cases, the secret to performance is hidden in the execution plan, revealing a missing index or so.

 It is recommended to pay special attention to situations where the number of expected rows seriously differs from the number of rows really processed. Keep in mind that the planner is usually right, but not always. Be cautious in case of large differences (especially if this input is fed into a nested loop).

Whenever a query feels slow, we always recommend to take a look at the plan first. In many cases, you will find missing indexes.

The internal structure of a B-tree index

Before we dig further into the B-tree indexes, we can briefly discuss what an index actually looks like under the hood.

Understanding the B-tree internals

Consider the following image that shows how things work:

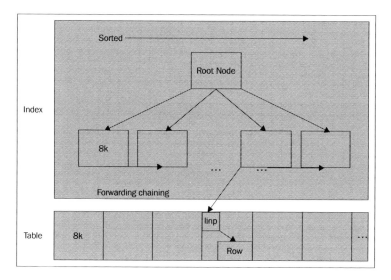

In PostgreSQL, we use the so-called Lehman-Yao B-trees (check out `http://www.cs.cmu.edu/~dga/15-712/F07/papers/Lehman81.pdf`). The main advantage of the B-trees is that they can handle concurrency very nicely. It is possible that hundreds or thousands of concurrent users modify the tree at the same time. Unfortunately, there is not enough room in this book to explain precisely how this works.

The two most important issues of this tree are the facts that I/O is done in 8,000 chunks and that the tree is actually a sorted structure. This allows PostgreSQL to apply a ton of optimizations.

Providing a sorted order

As we stated before, a B-tree provides the system with sorted output. This can come in quite handy. Here is a simple query to make use of the fact that a B-tree provides the system with sorted output:

```
test=# explain SELECT * FROM t_test ORDER BY id LIMIT 3;
                      QUERY PLAN
--------------------------------------------------------
 Limit  (cost=0.43..0.67 rows=3 width=9)
   ->  Index Scan using idx_id on t_test
  (cost=0.43..320094.43 rows=4000000 width=9)
(2 rows)
```

In this case, we are looking for the three smallest values. PostgreSQL will read the index from left to right and stop as soon as enough rows have been returned.

 This is a very common scenario. Many people think that indexes are only about searching, but this is not true. B-trees are also present to help out with sorting.

Why do you, the DBA, care about this stuff? Remember that this is a typical use case where a software developer comes to your desk, pounds on the table, and complains. A simple index can fix the problem.

Combined indexes

Combined indexes are one more source of trouble if they are not used properly. A combined index is an index covering more than one column.

Let's drop the existing index and create a combined index (make sure your seq_page_cost variable is set back to default to make the following examples work):

```
test=# DROP INDEX idx_combined;
DROP INDEX
test=# CREATE INDEX idx_combined ON t_test (name, id);
CREATE INDEX
```

We defined a composite index consisting of two columns. Remember that we put the name before the ID.

A simple query will return the following execution plan:

```
test=# explain analyze SELECT * FROM t_test
   WHERE id = 10;
                QUERY PLAN
--------------------------------------------------
 Seq Scan on t_test   (cost=0.00..71622.00 rows=1
   width=9)
   (actual time=181.502..351.439 rows=1 loops=1)
   Filter: (id = 10)
   Rows Removed by Filter: 3999999
 Total runtime: 351.481 ms
(4 rows)
```

There is no proper index for this, so the system will fall back to a sequential scan. Why is there no proper index? Well, try to look up for first names only in the telephone book. This is not going to work because a telephone book is sorted by location, last name, and first name. The same applies to our index. A B-tree works basically on the same principles as an ordinary paper phone book. It is only useful if you look up the first couple of values, or simply all of them. Here is an example:

```
test=# explain analyze SELECT * FROM t_test
   WHERE id = 10 AND name = 'joe';
      QUERY PLAN


-----------------------------------------------------------
 Index Only Scan using idx_combined on t_test
   (cost=0.43..6.20 rows=1 width=9)
  (actual time=0.068..0.068 rows=0 loops=1)
   Index Cond: ((name = 'joe'::text) AND (id = 10))
   Heap Fetches: 0
 Total runtime: 0.108 ms
(4 rows)
```

In this case, the combined index comes up with a high speed result of 0.1 ms, which is not bad.

After this small example, we can turn to an issue that's a little bit more complex. Let's change the costs of a sequential scan to 100-times normal:

```
test=# SET seq_page_cost TO 100;
SET
```

Don't let yourself be fooled into believing that an index is always good:

```
test=# explain analyze SELECT * FROM t_test
  WHERE id = 10;
                 QUERY PLAN
-----------------------------------------------------------
 Index Only Scan using idx_combined on t_test
  (cost=0.43..91620.44 rows=1 width=9)
  (actual time=0.362..177.952 rows=1 loops=1)
   Index Cond: (id = 10)
   Heap Fetches: 1
 Total runtime: 177.983 ms
(4 rows)
```

Just look at the execution times. We are almost as slow as a sequential scan here. Why does PostgreSQL use the index at all? Well, let's assume we have a very broad table. In this case, sequentially scanning the table is expensive. Even if we have to read the *entire* index, it can be cheaper than having to read the entire table, at least if there is enough hope to reduce the amount of data by using the index somehow. So, in case you see an index scan, also take a look at the execution times and the number of rows used. The index might not be perfect, but it's just an attempt by PostgreSQL to avoid the worse to come.

> Keep in mind that there is no general rule (for example, more than 25 percent of data will result in a sequential scan) for sequential scans. The plans depend on a couple of internal issues, such as physical disk layout (correlation) and so on.

Partial indexes

Up to now, an index covered the entire table. This is not always necessarily the case. There are also partial indexes. When is a partial index useful? Consider the following example:

```
test=# CREATE TABLE t_invoice (
    id      serial,
    d       date,
    amount    numeric,
    paid      boolean);
CREATE TABLE
test=# CREATE INDEX idx_partial
    ON   t_invoice (paid)
    WHERE   paid = false;
CREATE INDEX
```

In our case, we create a table storing invoices. We can safely assume that the majority of the invoices are nicely paid. However, we expect a minority to be pending, so we want to search for them. A partial index will do the job in a highly space efficient way. Space is important because saving on space has a couple of nice side effects, such as cache efficiency and so on.

Dealing with different types of indexes

Let's move on to an important issue: not everything can be sorted easily and in a useful way. Have you ever tried to sort circles? If the question seems odd, just try to do it. It will not be easy and will be highly controversial, so how do we do it best? Would we sort by size or coordinates? Under any circumstances, using a B-tree to store circles, points, or polygons might not be a good idea at all. A B-tree does not do what you want it to do because a B-tree depends on some kind of sorting order.

To provide end users with maximum flexibility and power, PostgreSQL provides more than just one index type. Each index type supports certain algorithms used for different purposes. The following list of index types is available in PostgreSQL (as of Version 9.4.1):

- `btree`: These are the high-concurrency B-trees
- `gist`: This is an index type for geometric searches (GIS data) and for KNN-search
- `gin`: This is an index type optimized for **Full-Text Search** (**FTS**)
- `sp-gist`: This is a space-partitioned gist

As we mentioned before, each type of index serves different purposes. We highly encourage you to dig into this extremely important topic to make sure that you can help software developers whenever necessary.

> Unfortunately, we don't have enough room in this book to discuss all the index types in greater depth. If you are interested in finding out more, we recommend checking out information on my website at http://www.postgresql-support.de/slides/2013_dublin_indexing.pdf.
>
> Alternatively, you can look up the official PostgreSQL documentation, which can be found at http://www.postgresql.org/docs/9.4/static/indexes.html.

Detecting missing indexes

Now that we have covered the basics and some selected advanced topics of indexing, we want to shift our attention to a major and highly important administrative task: hunting down missing indexes.

When talking about missing indexes, there is one essential query I have found to be highly valuable. The query is given as follows:

```
test=# \x
Expanded display (expanded) is on.
test=# SELECT   relname, seq_scan, seq_tup_read,
       idx_scan, idx_tup_fetch,
       seq_tup_read / seq_scan
  FROM   pg_stat_user_tables
  WHERE   seq_scan > 0
  ORDER BY seq_tup_read DESC;
-[ RECORD 1 ]-+---------
 relname       | t_user
 seq_scan      | 824350
 seq_tup_read  | 2970269443530
 idx_scan      | 0
 idx_tup_fetch | 0
 ?column?      | 3603165
```

The `pg_stat_user_tables` option contains statistical information about tables and their access patterns. In this example, we found a classic problem. The `t_user` table has been scanned close to 1 million times. During these sequential scans, we processed close to 3 trillion rows. Do you think this is unusual? It's not nearly as unusual as you might think.

In the last column, we divided `seq_tup_read` through `seq_scan`. Basically, this is a simple way to figure out how many rows a typical sequential scan has used to finish. In our case, 3.6 million rows had to be read. Do you remember our initial example? We managed to read 4 million rows in a couple of hundred milliseconds. So, it is absolutely realistic that nobody noticed the performance bottleneck before. However, just consider burning, say, 300 ms for every query thousands of times. This can easily create a heavy load on a totally unnecessary scale. In fact, a missing index is the key factor when it comes to bad performance.

Let's take a look at the table description now:

```
test=# \d t_user
                      Table "public.t_user"
  Column  |  Type   |            Modifiers
----------+---------+-------------------------------
 id       | integer | not null default
    nextval('t_user_id_seq'::regclass)
```

```
 email  | text  |
 passwd | text  |
Indexes:
    "t_user_pkey" PRIMARY KEY, btree (id)
```

This is really a classic example. It is hard to tell how often I have seen this kind of example in the field. The table was probably called `customer` or `userbase`. The basic principle of the problem was always the same: we got an index on the primary key, but the primary key was never checked during the authentication process. When you log in to Facebook, Amazon, Google, and so on, you will not use your internal ID, you will rather use your e-mail address. Therefore, it should be indexed.

The rules here are simple: we are searching for queries that needed many expensive scans. We don't mind sequential scans as long as they only read a handful of rows or as long as they show up rarely (caused by backups, for example). We need to keep expensive scans in mind, however ("expensive" in terms of "many rows needed").

Here is an example code snippet that should not bother us at all:

```
-[ RECORD 1 ]-+---------
 relname       | t_province
 seq_scan      | 8345345
 seq_tup_read  | 100144140
 idx_scan      | 0
 idx_tup_fetch | 0
 ?column?      | 12
```

The table has been read 8 million times, but in an average, only 12 rows have been returned. Even if we have 1 million indexes defined, PostgreSQL will not use them because the table is simply too small.

It is pretty hard to tell which columns might need an index from inside PostgreSQL. However, taking a look at the tables and thinking about them for a minute will, in most cases, solve the riddle. In many cases, things are pretty obvious anyway, and developers will be able to provide you with a reasonable answer.

As you can see, finding missing indexes is not hard, and we strongly recommend checking this system table once in a while to figure out whether your system works nicely.

There are a couple of tools, such as `pgbadger`, out there that can help us to monitor systems. It is recommended that you make use of such tools.

There is not only light, there is also some shadow. Indexes are not always good. They can also cause considerable overhead during writes. Keep in mind that when you insert, modify, or delete data, you have to touch the indexes as well. The overhead of useless indexes should never be underestimated. Therefore, it makes sense to not just look for missing indexes, but also for spare indexes that don't serve a purpose anymore.

Detecting slow queries

Now that we have seen how to hunt down tables that might need an index, we can move on to the next example and try to figure out the queries that cause most of the load on your system. Sometimes, the slowest query is not the one causing a problem; it is a bunch of small queries, which are executed over and over again. In this section, you will learn how to track down such queries.

To track down slow operations, we can rely on a module called `pg_stat_statements`. This module is available as part of the PostgreSQL `contrib` section. Installing a module from this section is really easy. Connect to PostgreSQL as a superuser, and execute the following instruction (if `contrib` packages have been installed):

```
test=# CREATE EXTENSION pg_stat_statements;
CREATE EXTENSION
```

This module will install a system view that will contain all the relevant information we need to find expensive operations:

```
test=# \d pg_stat_statements
        View "public.pg_stat_statements"
      Column        |       Type       | Modifiers
--------------------+------------------+-----------
 userid             | oid              |
 dbid               | oid              |
 queryid            | bigint           |
 query              | text             |
 calls              | bigint           |
 total_time         | double precision |
 rows               | bigint           |
 shared_blks_hit    | bigint           |
 shared_blks_read   | bigint           |
 shared_blks_dirtied | bigint          |
```

shared_blks_written	bigint	
local_blks_hit	bigint	
local_blks_read	bigint	
local_blks_dirtied	bigint	
local_blks_written	bigint	
temp_blks_read	bigint	
temp_blks_written	bigint	
blk_read_time	double precision	
blk_write_time	double precision	

In this view, we can see the queries we are interested in, the total execution time (`total_time`), the number of calls, and the number of rows returned. Then, we will get some information about the I/O behavior (more on caching later) of the query as well as information about temporary data being read and written. Finally, the last two columns will tell us how much time we actually spent on I/O. The final two fields are active when `track_timing` in `postgresql.conf` has been enabled and will give vital insights into potential reasons for disk wait and disk-related speed problems. The `blk_*` prefix will tell us how much time a certain query has spent reading and writing to the operating system.

Let's see what happens when we want to query the view:

```
test=# SELECT * FROM pg_stat_statements;
ERROR:  pg_stat_statements must be loaded via
    shared_preload_libraries
```

The system will tell us that we have to enable this module; otherwise, data won't be collected.

All we have to do to make this work is to add the following line to `postgresql.conf`:

```
shared_preload_libraries = 'pg_stat_statements'
```

Then, we have to restart the server to enable it. We highly recommend adding this module to the configuration straightaway to make sure that a restart can be avoided and that this data is always around.

> Don't worry too much about the performance overhead of this module. Tests have shown that the impact on performance is so low that it is even too hard to measure. Therefore, it might be a good idea to have this module activated all the time.

If you have configured things properly, finding the most time-consuming queries should be simple:

```
SELECT *
  FROM   pg_stat_statements
  ORDER  BY total_time DESC;
```

The important part here is that PostgreSQL can nicely group queries. For instance:

```
SELECT * FROM foo WHERE bar = 1;
SELECT * FROM foo WHERE bar = 2;
```

PostgreSQL will detect that this is just one type of query and replace the two numbers in the WHERE clause with a placeholder indicating that a parameter was used here.

Of course, you can also sort by any other criteria: highest I/O time, highest number of calls, or whatever. The pg_stat_statement function has it all, and things are available in a way that makes the data very easy and efficient to use.

How to reset statistics

Sometimes, it is necessary to reset the statistics. If you are about to track down a problem, resetting can be very beneficial. Here is how it works:

```
test=# SELECT pg_stat_reset();
 pg_stat_reset
---------------


(1 row)


test=# SELECT pg_stat_statements_reset();
 pg_stat_statements_reset
--------------------------


(1 row)
```

The pg_stat_reset command will reset the entire system statistics (for example, pg_stat_user_tables). The second call will wipe out pg_stat_statements.

Adjusting memory parameters

After we find the slow queries, we can do something about them. The first step is always to fix indexing and make sure that sane requests are sent to the database. If you are requesting stupid things from PostgreSQL, you can expect trouble. Once the basic steps have been performed, we can move on to the PostgreSQL memory parameters, which need some tuning.

Optimizing shared buffers

One of the most essential memory parameters is `shared_buffers`. What are shared buffers? Let's assume we are about to read a table consisting of 8,000 blocks. PostgreSQL will check if the buffer is already in cache (`shared_buffers`), and if it is not, it will ask the underlying operating system to provide the database with the missing 8,000 blocks. If we are lucky, the operating system has a cached copy of the block. If we are not so lucky, the operating system has to go to the disk system and fetch the data (worst case). So, the more data we have in cache, the more efficient we will be.

Setting `shared_buffers` to the right value is more art than science. The general guideline is that `shared_buffers` should consume 25 percent of memory, but not more than 16 GB. Very large shared buffer settings are known to cause suboptimal performance in some cases. It is also not recommended to starve the filesystem cache too much on behalf of the database system. Mentioning the guidelines does not mean that it is eternal law — you really have to see this as a guideline you can use to get started. Different settings might be better for your workload. Remember, if there was an eternal law, there would be no setting, but some autotuning magic. However, a `contrib` module called `pg_buffercache` can give some insights into what is in cache at the moment. It can be used as a basis to get started on understanding what is going on inside the PostgreSQL shared buffer.

Changing `shared_buffers` can be done in `postgresql.conf`, shown as follows:

```
shared_buffers = 4GB
```

In our example, shared buffers have been set to 4GB. A database restart is needed to activate the new value.

In PostgreSQL 9.4, some changes were introduced. Traditionally, PostgreSQL used a classical System V shared memory to handle the shared buffers. Starting with PostgreSQL 9.3, mapped memory was added, and finally, it was in PostgreSQL 9.4 that a `config` variable was introduced to configure the memory technique PostgreSQL will use, shown as follows:

```
dynamic_shared_memory_type = posix
  # the default is the first option
    # supported by the operating system:
    #   posix
    #   sysv
    #   windows
    #   mmap
    # use none to disable dynamic shared memory
```

The default value on the most common operating systems is basically fine. However, feel free to experiment with the settings and see what happens performance wise.

Considering huge pages

When a process uses RAM, the CPU marks this memory as used by this process. For efficiency reasons, the CPU usually allocates RAM by chunks of 4,000 bytes. These chunks are called **pages**. The process address space is virtual, and the CPU and operating system have to remember which process belongs to which page. The more pages you have, the more time it takes to find where the memory is mapped. When a process uses 1 GB of memory, it means that 262.144 blocks have to be looked up.

Most modern CPU architectures support bigger pages, and these pages are called **huge pages** (on Linux).

To tell PostgreSQL that this mechanism can be used, the following `config` variable can be changed in `postgresql.conf`:

```
huge_pages = try                    # on, off, or try
```

Of course, your Linux system has to know about the use of huge pages. Therefore, you can do some tweaking, as follows:

```
grep Hugepagesize /proc/meminfo
Hugepagesize:     2048 kB
```

In our case, the size of the huge pages is 2 MB. So, if there is 1 GB of memory, 512 huge pages are needed.

The number of huge pages can be configured and activated by setting `nr_hugepages` in the `proc` filesystem. Consider the following example:

```
echo 512 > /proc/sys/vm/nr_hugepages
```

Alternatively, we can use the `sysctl` command or change things in `/etc/sysctl.conf`:

```
sysctl -w vm.nr_hugepages=512
```

Huge pages can have a significant impact on performance.

Tweaking work_mem

There is more to PostgreSQL memory configuration than just shared buffers. The `work_mem` parameter is widely used for operations such as sorting, aggregating, and so on.

Let's illustrate the way `work_mem` works with a short, easy-to-understand example. Let's assume it is an election day and three parties have taken part in the elections.

The data is as follows:

```
test=# CREATE TABLE t_election (id serial, party text);
test=# INSERT INTO t_election (party)
  SELECT 'socialists'
    FROM generate_series(1, 439784);
test=# INSERT INTO t_election (party)
  SELECT 'conservatives'
    FROM generate_series(1, 802132);
test=# INSERT INTO t_election (party)
  SELECT 'liberals'
    FROM generate_series(1, 654033);
```

We add some data to the table and try to count how many votes each party has:

```
test=# explain analyze SELECT party, count(*)
    FROM    t_election
    GROUP BY 1;
        QUERY PLAN
-------------------------------------------------
```

```
HashAggregate  (cost=39461.24..39461.26 rows=3
    width=11) (actual time=609.456..609.456
   rows=3 loops=1)
   Group Key: party
  -> Seq Scan on t_election  (cost=0.00..29981.49
   rows=1895949 width=11)
   (actual time=0.007..192.934 rows=1895949
   loops=1)
 Planning time: 0.058 ms
 Execution time: 609.481 ms
(5 rows)
```

First of all, the system will perform a sequential scan and read all the data. This data is passed on to a so-called `HashAggregate`. For each party, PostgreSQL will calculate a hash key and increment counters as the query moves through the tables. At the end of the operation, we will have a chunk of memory with three values and three counters. Very nice! As you can see, the `explain analyze` statement does not take more than 600 ms.

> Note that the real execution time of the query will be a lot faster. The `explain analyze` statement does have some serious overhead. Still, it will give you valuable insights into the inner workings of the query.

Let's try to repeat this same example, but this time, we want to group by the ID. Here is the execution plan:

```
test=# explain analyze SELECT id, count(*)
    FROM   t_election
    GROUP BY 1;
        QUERY PLAN
-----------------------------------------------------
 GroupAggregate  (cost=253601.23..286780.33 rows=1895949
    width=4) (actual time=1073.769..1811.619
    rows=1895949 loops=1)
    Group Key: id
  -> Sort  (cost=253601.23..258341.10 rows=1895949
    width=4) (actual time=1073.763..1288.432
    rows=1895949 loops=1)
```

```
        Sort Key: id

        Sort Method: external sort  Disk: 25960kB

        ->  Seq Scan on t_election

    (cost=0.00..29981.49 rows=1895949 width=4)        (actual
time=0.013..235.046 rows=1895949

      loops=1)
 Planning time: 0.086 ms

 Execution time: 1928.573 ms

(8 rows)
```

The execution time rises by almost 2 seconds and, more importantly, the plan changes. In this scenario, there is no way to stuff all the 1.9 million hash keys into a chunk of memory because we are limited by work_mem. Therefore, PostgreSQL has to find an alternative plan. It will sort the data and run GroupAggregate. How does it work? If you have a sorted list of data, you can count all equal values; send them off to the client, and move on to the next value. The main advantage is that we don't have to keep the entire result set in memory at once. With GroupAggregate, we can basically return aggregations of infinite sizes. The downside is that large aggregates exceeding memory will create temporary files leading to potential disk I/O.

 Keep in mind that we are talking about the size of the result set and not about the size of the underlying data.

Let's try the same thing with more work_mem:

```
test=# SET work_mem TO '1 GB';

SET

test=# explain analyze SELECT id, count(*)

    FROM t_election

    GROUP BY 1;

        QUERY PLAN

----------------------------------------------------

 HashAggregate  (cost=39461.24..58420.73 rows=1895949

    width=4) (actual time=857.554..1343.375

    rows=1895949 loops=1)

   Group Key: id

   ->  Seq Scan on t_election  (cost=0.00..29981.49

    rows=1895949 width=4)

    (actual time=0.010..201.012
```

```
    rows=1895949 loops=1)
 Planning time: 0.113 ms
 Execution time: 1478.820 ms
(5 rows)
```

In this case, we adapted `work_mem` for the current session. Don't worry; changing `work_mem` locally does not change the parameter for other database connections. If you want to change things globally, you have to do so by changing things in `postgresql.conf`. Alternatively, 9.4 offers a command called `ALTER SYSTEM SET work_mem TO '1 GB'`. Once `SELECT pg_reload_conf()` has been called, the `config` parameter is changed as well.

What you see in this example is that the execution time is around half a second lower than before. PostgreSQL switches back to the more efficient plan.

However, there is more; `work_mem` is also in charge of efficient sorting:

```
test=# explain analyze SELECT * FROM t_election ORDER BY id DESC;
      QUERY PLAN

----------------------------------------------------
 Sort (cost=227676.73..232416.60 rows=1895949 width=15)
    (actual time=695.004..872.698 rows=1895949
    loops=1)
    Sort Key: id
    Sort Method: quicksort  Memory: 163092kB
    ->  Seq Scan on t_election  (cost=0.00..29981.49
    rows=1895949 width=15) (actual time=0.013..188.876
  rows=1895949 loops=1)
 Planning time: 0.042 ms
 Execution time: 995.327 ms
(6 rows)
```

In our example, PostgreSQL can sort the entire dataset in memory. Earlier, we had to perform a so-called "`external sort Disk`", which is way slower because temporary results have to be written to disk.

The `work_mem` command is used for some other operations as well. However, sorting and aggregation are the most common use cases.

Keep in mind that `work_mem` should not be abused, and `work_mem` can be allocated to every sorting or grouping operation. So, more than just one `work_mem` amount of memory might be allocated by a single query.

Improving maintenance_work_mem

To control the memory consumption of administrative tasks, PostgreSQL offers a parameter called `maintenance_work_mem`. It is used to handle index creations as well as VACUUM.

Usually, creating an index (B-tree) is mostly related to sorting, and the idea of `maintenance_work_mem` is to speed things up. However, things are not as simple as they might seem. People might assume that increasing the parameter will always speed things up, but this is not necessarily true; in fact, smaller values might even be beneficial. We conducted some research to solve this riddle. The in-depth results of this research can be found at `http://www.cybertec.at/ adjusting-maintenance_work_mem/`.

However, indexes are not the only beneficiaries. The `maintenance_work_mem` command is also here to help VACUUM clean out indexes. If `maintenance_work_mem` is too low, you might see VACUUM scanning tables repeatedly because dead items cannot be stored in memory during VACUUM. This is something that should basically be avoided.

Just like all other memory parameters, `maintenance_work_mem` can be set per session, or it can be set globally in `postgresql.conf`.

Adjusting effective_cache_size

The number of `shared_buffers` assigned to PostgreSQL is not the only cache in the system. The operating system will also cache data and do a great job of improving speed. To make sure that the PostgreSQL optimizer knows what to expect from the operation system, `effective_cache_size` has been introduced. The idea is to tell PostgreSQL how much cache there is going to be around (*shared buffers + operating system side cache*). The optimizer can then adjust its costs and estimates to reflect this knowledge.

It is recommended to always set this parameter; otherwise, the planner might come up with suboptimal plans.

Summary

In this chapter, you learned how to detect basic performance bottlenecks. In addition to this, we covered the very basics of the PostgreSQL optimizer and indexes. At the end of the chapter, some important memory parameters were presented.

In the next chapter, we will dig into user management and user permissions; some important aspects related to security will also be discussed.

3
Users and Permissions

This chapter is all about users and permissions. You will be guided through the essential concepts and ideas of the PostgreSQL security system.

In this chapter, you will learn the following topics:

- Network security
- Users and roles
- Common pitfalls
- Securing procedures
- Managing SSL
- Using SELinux

Understanding PostgreSQL security

In this section, you will learn about the basic PostgreSQL security model. In general, we can see the PostgreSQL security models as seven basic layers:

- **Level 1**: Turning the TCP on or off (`listen_addresses` in `postgresql.conf`, and so on)
- **Level 2**: Network authentication (`pg_hba.conf`)
- **Level 3**: Instance-level permissions
- **Level 4**: Database-level permissions
- **Level 5**: Schema-level permissions
- **Level 6**: Table-level permissions
- **Level 7**: Column permissions

Of course, there is more than just permissions on these seven levels; however, most administrators will face exactly those seven stages when securing their systems. So, let us go through these steps in detail and discuss each of them separately.

Configuring the TCP

The first thing you have to do while securing a database instance is to take care of the network security. One of the useful features here is that you can make PostgreSQL take certain network addresses into consideration or just ignore them.

Note that we are talking about *your* network addresses here—so, addresses bound to one of your network devices. Technically, it means that you can use this feature to actually ignore the entire network devices.

The important variable in this context is `listen_addresses` in `postgresql.conf`, which shown as follows:

```
listen_addresses = 'localhost'
     # what IP address(es) to listen on;
     # comma-separated list of addresses;
     # defaults to 'localhost'; use '*' for all
     # (change requires restart)
```

In our example, we have listed the default settings of PostgreSQL on Linux. What do these default settings actually mean? It means that PostgreSQL will *only* listen to the local interfaces (namely local Unix sockets and the loopback device). The network devices will be totally ignored. If you try to reach PostgreSQL from a remote node, you will simply not see an open socket.

In other words, without changing `listen_addresses`, there is no way to connect to PostgreSQL from a remote box.

So, what if we want remote access? Let us assume we have a network device in our service listening on `192.168.0.3` (the IP address of eth0, for example). We can do the following:

```
listen_addresses = '192.168.0.3'
```

In this case, this network interface is taken into consideration. Keep in mind that this setting is not about the client IPs—it is about your server IPs.

If you change the `listen_addresses` variable, you will have to restart PostgreSQL.

Managing network authentication

Once you have defined the basic TCP usage, we can move on and take care of pg_hba.conf, which is an essential component of every security system.

The idea of pg_hba.conf is as follows: when a request comes in, PostgreSQL will apply different rules of authentication depending on the origin of the request. For example, you might want to establish the following policies:

- Users connecting to PostgreSQL from the database server should not need a password

- Users connecting from within the same server rack should require a password

- Users connecting from the computing center across the street should use LDAP for authentication

- Users connecting from some other countries are forced to use SSL and a valid username

The pg_hba.conf file is exactly what you have been looking for because you can define exactly those rules outlined in this little listing. Consider the following example of a simple pg_hba.conf file:

```
# TYPE   DATABASE USER    ADDRESS            METHOD


# "local" is for Unix domain socket connections only
local   all      all                        trust


# IPv4 local connections:
host    all      all     127.0.0.1/32       trust


# IPv6 local connections
host    all      all     ::1/128            trust


# remote access
host    all      all     192.168.0.0/16     md5
host    all      all     213.43.13.0/24     pam
```

This is a typical example of a standard pg_hba.conf configuration. We allow local users coming through Unix sockets to enter the database without a password (this is what *trust* does). By the way—that's the reason why PostgreSQL has not asked us for a password so far when we connected to the system.

The second and the third lines indicate that IPv4 and IPv6 connections coming from the local system will also not require a password. In fact, the first three lines just make sure that our local system is marked as trustworthy as possible.

Then, we can focus our intention on the remote access: whenever somebody tries to connect from 192.168.*.*, PostgreSQL will ask for a password. The md5 authentication method is in charge of asking for a netmask and /16 represents the netmask. The netmask will define the size of the subnet we want to allow. The md5 authentication method is pretty common in real-world scenarios.

Finally, we want to open one more IP range for the external users. In our example, a small specialty is used: the pam authentication method allows PostgreSQL to rely on the operating system meant for authentication. The **Pluggable Authentication Module (PAM)** is a central component of (not only) Linux and allows all kinds of trickery. For more information about PAM, consult the PAM website at http://www.linux-pam.org/Linux-PAM-html/.

> We are talking about authentication here. If you use PAM in combination with, say, Microsoft Active Directory, adding a user to the Active Directory is not enough to make this work. A user must be in PostgreSQL, as well as in Active Directory. After all, we are only talking about authentication here and not about external user management.

If you want to use PAM, two things have to be considered:

- PostgreSQL has to be compiled using --with-pam (binary packages are usually made this way to figure out you can call pg_config and check in detail).
- The default PAM service name is postgresql, so you have to create this file in the appropriate place to make this work. On many Linux distros, the proper directory is /etc/pam.d.

Managing contradictions

There is more. You can also lock people out from the system. If you want to block an IP, you can utilize reject. Consider the following example:

```
host    all    all    192.168.34.165/32  reject
```

As you can see in the previous code snippet, `reject` is the magic word here. It will make sure that this IP has no chance. But, what if rules contradict each other? Consider the following example:

```
host    all    all    192.168.0.0/16       md5
host    all    all    192.168.34.165/32  reject
```

In this example, an entire range has been opened. Then, we want to reject a single IP within this range. What is going to happen? The golden rule here is: the first rule matching will be taken. So, if somebody tries to connect from 192.168.34.165, he/she will hit the first rule. Of course, this rule matches so the connection will be allowed and the user can potentially get in. In the given example, the second rule is simply useless as it is already handled by the first rule.

To get this right, we have to reorder both the lines as follows:

```
host    all    all    192.168.34.165/32  reject
host    all    all    192.168.0.0/16       md5
```

In this case, `reject` is hit first. PostgreSQL stops the process and the IP is excluded from the range.

Authentication methods available

Until now we have dealt with `trust`, `reject`, `md5`, and `pam`. But there is more. PostgreSQL provides us with a variety of authentication methods. The following listing shows which methods are available as of PostgreSQL 9.4:

- `trust`: This method makes sure that an IP or an IP range can access the database without a password. Of course, you will need a valid user for this (on some systems this is the default).

- `reject`: This method bans an IP range from the server (by default everybody is blocked and so `pg_hba.conf` entries are important to allow remote access).

- `md5`: This method asks the user for a password and will send the password over the network encrypted.

- `password`: This authentication method is rarely used these days because it sends passwords in plain texts. It is highly recommended to use `md5` or some other method instead.

- gss: GSSAPI is an industry-standard protocol as defined in RFC2743. This setting is mainly used in conjunction with the Kerberos authentication. To use this feature, PostgreSQL must be compiled with --with-gssapi. If GSSAPI is used along with Kerberos, the default Kerberos server name can be changed by adding --with-krb-srvnam to the build process.

- sspi: If you happen to be in a Windows environment, you can choose sspi. It is a Windows technology for single-sign-on. PostgreSQL will use SSPI in negotiate mode, which will use Kerberos when possible and automatically fall back to NTLM in other cases. Keep in mind that SSPI authentication only works when both the server and the client are running on Windows or on non-Windows platforms, when GSSAPI is available.

- ident: With the ident authentication, the client's operating system username is obtained and used for the login process. It only works in TCP/IP connections.

- peer: This works by obtaining the client's username from the kernel and using it for authentication. Be aware that this only works for local connections. In many distributions, this is the default authentication method.

- ldap: LDAP is widely used for central authentication. The idea is that PostgreSQL will consult an LDAP server to check if a certain user is valid or not.

- radius: Radius, LDAP, and password work in a similar way. The only difference is that Radius is called instead of LDAP. The irony here is that you can use PostgreSQL as a backend database for Radius as well.

- cert: With this authentication method, SSL client certificates are used for authentication. Logically cert only works with SSL-encrypted connections.

- pam: Finally, PAM provides you with all the methods available on Linux, Solaris, and so on, which have not been listed here. By providing a PAM configuration, you can add even more functionality.

The pg_hba.conf file can be made arbitrarily complex. However, keep in mind that the database is not a firewall. It is recommended to keep things simple and easy to understand. Otherwise mistakes can easily happen.

Some more examples

Until now, some basic pg_hba.conf examples have been discussed. In addition to that, overview of those authentication methods have been provided. However, not all authentication methods are as simple to use as trust, reject, md5, and password.

Some of the authentication methods such as LDAP, GSSAPI, and so on need some more information to function properly. Here are two of the LDAP examples:

```
host    all     all     192.168.1.0/24      ldap
  ldapserver=ldap.cybertec.at ldapprefix="cn="
  ldapsuffix=", dc=example, dc=net"


host    all     all     192.168.2.0/24      ldap
  ldapserver=ldap.postgresql-support.de
  ldapbasedn="dc=example, dc=net"
  ldapsearchattribute=uid
```

To use LDAP for authentication, PostgreSQL has to know where to look for the LDAP server in charge. This kind of information has to be passed on in this authentication option.

> Make sure that your `pg_hba.conf` entries are one liners. Line breaks have just been added to make things more readable in print.

For a detailed explanation of all authentication methods, check out the following website: `http://www.postgresql.org/docs/9.4/interactive/auth-methods.html`

Handling SSL

Many users rely on unencrypted database connections. However, in many cases, it is just not possible to rely on unencrypted communications. For security reasons, encryption can be highly beneficial. In this section, we will be discussing using SSL with PostgreSQL.

The first thing to do is to make sure that PostgreSQL has been compiled using `--with-openssl`. Here's how you create a self-signed `cert` on a Unix-style system with OpenSSL installed:

```
openssl req -new -text -out server.req
```

Answer the questions during the creation process. Make sure you enter the localhost name as `Common Name`; the challenge password can be left blank. The program will generate a key that is passphrase protected. Keep in mind that the passphrase must be at least four characters long.

Once the key has been generated, run the following command:

```
chmod og-rwx server.key
```

Then, copy the file to the directory where PostgreSQL will look for it. Usually, this is the $PGDATA directory (the home directory of the instance).

However, these paths can be changed: ssl_cert_file, ssl_key_file, ssl_ca_file, and ssl_crl_file are postgresql.conf parameters, defining where PostgreSQL will look for those keys.

Once the keys have been made and put into $PGDATA, you can put the hostssl records into pg_hba.conf.

The ssl configuration option must be set in postgresql.conf.

Changing pg_hba.conf

It might happen from time to time that pg_hba.conf has to be changed. Don't worry—there is no need to restart the entire database server in this case. It is totally sufficient to perform the following command:

```
pg_ctl -D … reload
```

Behind the scenes, a signal (SIGHUP) will be sent to the server. Of course, it is also possible to do this through init scripts. Depending on your infrastructure and setup, /etc/init.d might be a good start (the name of the service might vary, of course, especially if more than one instance is on the same server):

```
/etc/init.d/postgresql reload
```

If you don't want to go through the init script, you can also do it the plain-metal Unix way:

```
root@chantal:~# ps ax | grep postgresql
 1603 ?          S          0:11 /usr/local/pgsql/bin/postgres
           -D /data
 1726 pts/0      S+         0:00 grep --color=auto postgresql
root@chantal:~# kill -HUP 1603
```

Just extract the process ID from the process and send the signal by invoking the kill command. Alternatively, you can call SELECT pg_reload_conf().

From now on, all new authentication attempts will use the new configuration. Existing database connections will be unharmed.

Handling instance-level permissions

After taking care of the first two levels of security (`listen_addresses` in `postgresql.conf` and `pg_hba.conf`), it is time to discuss the PostgreSQL user concept. The first important piece of information is that in PostgreSQL users are always a property of an instance. It is not something contained by a single database inside the instance.

The second important fact is the notion of roles. Many years ago PostgreSQL was based on a Unix-like user/group/world-concept. However, this has been extended to a role-based concept. The idea is simple and can be summed up in two central axioms:

- Users, groups, and roles are the very same thing (called roles)
- Roles can be nested indefinitely

The fact that roles can be nested opens a variety of opportunities to make things highly flexible.

Creating roles

Before moving on to the issues, it is time to take a look at the syntax of CREATE ROLE:

```
test=# \h CREATE ROLE
Command:      CREATE ROLE
Description: define a new database role
Syntax:
CREATE ROLE name [ [ WITH ] option [ ... ] ]


where option can be:


    SUPERUSER | NOSUPERUSER
  | CREATEDB | NOCREATEDB
  | CREATEROLE | NOCREATEROLE
  | CREATEUSER | NOCREATEUSER
  | INHERIT | NOINHERIT
  | LOGIN | NOLOGIN
  | REPLICATION | NOREPLICATION
  | CONNECTION LIMIT connlimit
  | [ ENCRYPTED | UNENCRYPTED ] PASSWORD 'password'
  | VALID UNTIL 'timestamp'
  | IN ROLE role_name [, ...]
```

```
    |   IN GROUP role_name [, ...]
    |   ROLE role_name [, ...]
    |   ADMIN role_name [, ...]
    |   USER role_name [, ...]
    |   SYSID uid
```

If you issue a \h CREATE USER command, you will see that the syntax is absolutely identical because it is the very same thing anyway.

The syntax is actually quite simple. Here is how those various clauses work:

- SUPERUSER | NOSUPERUSER: This setting defines whether a user is a superuser or not. Keep in mind that you cannot take permissions (on tables or so) away from a superuser. A superuser will be able to do whatever he/she pleases to do. It is only possible to restrict a superuser by turning him/her into a non-superuser. Here, NOSUPERUSER is the default value.

- CREATEDB | NOCREATEDB: This clause allows a user (role) to create a database inside the database instance. If a new database is created, the creator will also automatically be the owner. Here, NOCREATEDB is the default value.

- CREATEROLE | NOCREATEROLE: This clause allows creating, dropping, or modifying a role. Here, NOCREATEROLE is the default value.

- CREATEUSER | NOCREATEUSER: These clauses are an obsolete, but still accepted, spelling of SUPERUSER and NOSUPERUSER. Note that they are not equivalent to CREATEROLE as one might naively expect.

- INHERIT | NOINHERIT: This clause controls whether a role can inherit rights from other roles or not. Here, INHERIT is the default value.

- LOGIN | NOLOGIN: Can somebody log in to the instance or not? This is the main key to the instance. Logging in to the instance is not enough to make it into a database yet, but it is a precondition. Here, NOLOGIN is the default.

- REPLICATION | NOREPLICATION: If you are using streaming replication, the slave does not have to connect to its master as a superuser. It is enough if you create an unprivileged user capable of streaming. The REPLICATION clause helps to secure your replication setup. Here, NOREPLICATION is the default.

- CONNECTION LIMIT: This clause defines how many concurrent open connections a user is allowed to have. By default, there is no limitation for a user.

- PASSWORD: Passwords can be encrypted or unencrypted. Of course, encrypted passwords are the default. However, unencrypted passwords can come in handy when a system is developed or tested—you can look up unencrypted passwords in the system catalog.

- VALID UNTIL: If a role is only allowed to operate until a given point in time, VALID UNTIL can be very helpful because the validity of a user can be restricted. It makes sure that you cannot forget to lock a user again after a given period of time.

- IN ROLE | IN GROUP: This clause will list the roles of a member of a certain role. The IN ROLE clause is the new syntax and IN GROUP is obsolete and should not be used anymore.

- ROLE: This clause lists the roles you want to inherit from.

- ADMIN: This clause is like ROLE but roles are added with WITH ADMIN OPTION automatically.

- USER: This clause is obsolete.

- SYSID: This clause is ignored but it is still around for backward compatibility.

After this extensive introduction, it is time to actually create a role and see things in action:

```
test=# CREATE ROLE accountant NOLOGIN NOSUPERUSER NOCREATEDB;
CREATE ROLE
test=# CREATE ROLE joseph LOGIN NOSUPERUSER NOCREATEDB;
CREATE ROLE
test=# GRANT accountant TO joseph;
GRANT ROLE
```

Direct use of the role concept is made in this example: in the first line a role called accountant is created. The important part here is that the role is marked as NOLOGIN. Logically, PostgreSQL won't let us in as accountant, as shown in the following code:

```
hs@chantal:~$ psql test -U accountant
psql: FATAL:  role "accountant" is not permitted to log in
```

But, it is possible to log in as joseph:

```
hs@chantal:~$ psql test -U joseph
psql (9.4.1)
Type "help" for help.
test=>
```

The role concept opens an interesting approach here. Let us assume that tasks are more stable than staff. What does it mean? Even in 10 years a company will employ an accountant but is it going to be the same person all the time? Or just somebody else? Nobody knows. What is certain, however, is the fact that the kind of work performed will most likely be the same (accounting). The role concept is wonderful here because we can build NOLOGIN roles built on tasks and assign those tasks to real people then. There is no need to assign rights to a person straightaway—going through a role adds a highly convenient layer of abstraction here.

 Note that the prompt has changed slightly. The => sign indicates that the user connected to the database is not a superuser.

Finally, accountant is granted to joseph. In other words, joseph will now inherit all rights from accountant. If new rights are assigned to accountant, joseph will automatically have those.

 Note that in PostgreSQL there can never be contradictions in the permission system. You can either have something or you can lack something. There is only an *allowed* list—there is no such thing as a *denied* list. Denied simply means that somebody does not have a right. Therefore, permissions are simply added up and there can never be contradictions.

Modifying and dropping roles

Once a role has been created, it can be modified easily. The ALTER ROLE clause gives us all the options needed here:

```
test=# \h ALTER ROLE
Command:     ALTER ROLE
Description: change a database role
Syntax:
ALTER ROLE name [ [ WITH ] option [ ... ] ]


where option can be:

      SUPERUSER | NOSUPERUSER
    | CREATEDB | NOCREATEDB
    | CREATEROLE | NOCREATEROLE
```

```
     |  CREATEUSER  |  NOCREATEUSER
     |  INHERIT  |  NOINHERIT
     |  LOGIN  |  NOLOGIN
     |  REPLICATION  |  NOREPLICATION
     |  CONNECTION LIMIT connlimit
     |  [ ENCRYPTED  |  UNENCRYPTED ] PASSWORD 'password'
     |  VALID UNTIL 'timestamp'


ALTER ROLE name RENAME TO new_name


ALTER ROLE name [ IN DATABASE database_name ] SET
  configuration_parameter { TO | = }
  { value | DEFAULT }
ALTER ROLE { name | ALL } [ IN DATABASE database_name ]
  SET configuration_parameter FROM CURRENT
ALTER ROLE { name | ALL } [ IN DATABASE database_name ]
  RESET configuration_parameter
ALTER ROLE { name | ALL } [ IN DATABASE database_name ]
    RESET ALL
```

Basically, everything supported by CREATE ROLE is also supported here. If you want to change a role from NOLOGIN to LOGIN, you can simply use:

```
ALTER ROLE foo LOGIN;
```

You can also change runtime parameters such as work_mem and so on by utilizing ALTER ROLE ... IN DATABASE ... SET ....

Consider the following example:

```
test=# ALTER DATABASE test SET work_mem TO '128 MB';
ALTER DATABASE
```

To drop a role, the following command has to be used:

```
test=# \h DROP ROLE
Command:     DROP ROLE
Description: remove a database role
Syntax:
DROP ROLE [ IF EXISTS ] name [, ...]
```

The IF EXISTS clause is pretty useful and noteworthy here because it makes use of DROP ROLE inside a transaction a lot easier. If a role does not exist, you will receive a warning and not an error—therefore, an open transaction can proceed without any problems.

Sometimes, it is not possible to drop a role straightaway. The reason can be quite simple: if a role still owns objects, dropping the role is impossible. It would not be PostgreSQL if there wasn't an easy solution to the problem. The command coming to our rescue is REASSIGN, as shown in the following command:

```
test=# \h REASSIGN
Command:     REASSIGN OWNED
Description: change the ownership of database
  objects owned by a database role
Syntax:
REASSIGN OWNED BY old_role [, ...] TO new_role
```

Once all objects have been reassigned, a role can be dropped quickly and safely.

Controlling database-level permissions

Roles, database creation, and all that are an issue at the instance level. Now, we can dig a little deeper and see how permissions can be assigned on the database level. At this stage, it is time to introduce GRANT. In general, GRANT is a powerful tool capable of handling object permissions. It allows setting all kinds of permission. In case permissions on databases have to be defined, the following syntax is available:

```
GRANT { { CREATE | CONNECT | TEMPORARY | TEMP } [, ...] | ALL [
PRIVILEGES ] }
    ON DATABASE database_name [, ...]
    TO { [ GROUP ] role_name | PUBLIC } [, ...]
  [ WITH GRANT OPTION ]
```

Two permissions are available on the database level: CREATE and CONNECT. The clue here is that once we have made it into the database instance (LOGIN is required to do so), we might not be allowed to connect to every single database in the system. A role might only be allowed to connect to 3 out of 10 databases.

Until now, joseph is still able to connect to the test database. Why is that so? The reason is that on PostgreSQL there is a parameter called *public*. The *public* parameter is allowed to connect to all databases. So, to make full use of those CONNECT rights, we have to make sure that the public is restricted first. To remove rights the REVOKE command is available:

```
test=# REVOKE ALL ON DATABASE test FROM public;
REVOKE
test=# \q
hs@chantal:~$ psql test -U joseph
psql: FATAL:  permission denied for database "test"
DETAIL:  User does not have CONNECT privilege.
```

Once public has been restricted, we can assign rights explicitly to joseph to make things work for joseph and the superusers only:

```
test=# GRANT CONNECT ON DATABASE test TO joseph;
GRANT
```

The user joseph can connect easily now.

The second permission available on the database level is CREATE. Usually, this permission leads to some misconceptions and confusion. The CREATE clause does *not* mean that you can create tables inside the database. It is all about schemas and not about tables. So, when somebody is allowed to *create*, schemas can be created.

Understanding schema-level permissions

The fact that CREATE is all about schemas takes us directly to the next level of security. PostgreSQL provides a functionality called **schemas**.

Let us see what happens if joseph tries to create a schema:

```
test=> CREATE SCHEMA sales;
ERROR:  permission denied for database test
```

As expected by most people, a normal, nonsuperuser is not allowed to create a schema. However, something unexpected is possible, as shown in the following code:

```
test=> CREATE TABLE t_disaster (id int4);
CREATE TABLE
test=> \d
         List of relations
 Schema |     Name     | Type  | Owner
--------+--------------+-------+--------
 public | t_disaster   | table | joseph
(1 row)
```

Any role can create a table. The table will end up in the so-called `public` schema, which is part of every single database in PostgreSQL.

How does PostgreSQL know where to put the table? The answer to this question lies in a variable called `search_path`, shown as follows:

```
test=> SHOW search_path;
  search_path
----------------
"$user",public
(1 row)
```

When a new table is created without an explicit prefix, PostgreSQL will take `search_path` and figure out where to put the table. In our example, there is no schema carrying the name of the current user, so PostgreSQL will fall back to the public schema listed second in `search_path`. As mentioned earlier, the public schema is indeed public.

 $user is very handy because it makes sure that a table always goes to a schema carrying the same name as the user. $user can also help to model Oracle-style behavior. In Oracle, a user is a lot more related to a schema than in PostgreSQL.

Most DBAs close this little loophole using the following SQL (run this one as superuser):

```
test=# REVOKE ALL ON SCHEMA public FROM public;
REVOKE
```

In the following case, `joseph` cannot do nasty stuff anymore:

```
test=> CREATE TABLE t_no_way (id int);
ERROR:  no schema has been selected to create in
test=> CREATE TABLE public.t_no_way (id int);
ERROR:  permission denied for schema public
```

When trying to create the table, an error message will be issued because PostgreSQL does not know where to put the table. In the second example, an explicit permission denied message will pop up.

Once this central loophole has been closed, it is time to focus our attention on the permissions we can set on a schema, as shown in the following command:

```
GRANT { { CREATE | USAGE } [, ...]
```

```
  | ALL [ PRIVILEGES ] }
    ON SCHEMA schema_name [, ...]
      TO { [ GROUP ] role_name | PUBLIC } [, ...]
  [ WITH GRANT OPTION ]
```

Again, two permissions are available. The CREATE clause will allow us to put objects (such as tables) into a schema. The USAGE clause will allow us to actually look into a schema and see which objects are present.

Here is an example showing how a superuser can create a schema and allow all accountants in:

```
test=# CREATE SCHEMA sales;
CREATE SCHEMA
test=# GRANT CREATE ON SCHEMA sales TO accountant;
GRANT
test=# \q
```

All the roles inheriting from accountant will be allowed to put objects into the sales schema now. Here is the proof:

```
hs@chantal:~$ psql test -U joseph
psql (9.4.1)
Type "help" for help.
test=> CREATE TABLE sales.t_sales (id int4);
CREATE TABLE
```

Once we have covered schemas, we can move on to table permissions.

Handling table-level permissions

To many users, tables are the central component of a relational database. Therefore, PostgreSQL offers a variety of permissions, which can be set for a specific table. The next listing shows which syntax elements are available:

```
GRANT { { SELECT | INSERT | UPDATE | DELETE | TRUNCATE
    | REFERENCES | TRIGGER }
  [, ...] | ALL [ PRIVILEGES ] }
    ON { [ TABLE ] table_name [, ...]
        | ALL TABLES IN SCHEMA schema_name [, ...] }
      TO { [ GROUP ] role_name | PUBLIC } [, ...]
  [ WITH GRANT OPTION ]
```

The following permissions can be set:

- SELECT: This permission allows users to read rows in a table.
- INSERT: This permission allows users to add data to a table. Keep in mind that INSERT does not imply SELECT. It is absolutely possible to be able to write but not read.
- UPDATE: This permission allows users to change data.
- DELETE: This permission allows users to delete data.
- TRUNCATE: The DELETE and TRUNCATE permissions are two distinct components. As the latter requires a lot more locking, these two permissions are available here.
- REFERENCES: Can a table be referenced or not? This permission allows a user to create foreign-key constraints.
- TRIGGER: This permission allows the creation of triggers.

As you can see, PostgreSQL allows you to set a variety of different permissions here. It is especially worth investigating REFERENCES a little closer. Let us assume that you have two tables: t_user and t_disease (1:n). If a person adds a disease to the t_disease table, it might be beneficial to make sure that he/she cannot see more than the sick person's ID in t_user. You might really want to prevent people from knowing who has which sickness. The REFERENCES component makes sure that a foreign key can exist but will also make sure that t_user cannot be read in its entirety.

It is also recommended to check out the ALL TABLES IN SCHEMA clause. If you want to assign the same rights to all tables within a schema, this is a handy way to reduce your workload.

Finally, there is the WITH GRANT OPTION clause. Suppose a database instance hosts 200 users, the administrator might not be able to take care of each of them. So, permissions can be passed on by the superuser to other people using WITH GRANT OPTION. Having a GRANT option means that permissions can be passed-on on the behalf of the DBA—what a neat way to spread the workload of administrating user permissions.

Managing column rights

Finally, it is time to move on to level 7: column permissions. The following syntax is available for column permissions:

```
GRANT { { SELECT | INSERT | UPDATE | REFERENCES }
  ( column_name [, ...] )
    [, ...] | ALL [ PRIVILEGES ]
  ( column_name [, ...] ) }
    ON [ TABLE ] table_name [, ...]
    TO { [ GROUP ] role_name | PUBLIC } [, ...]
  [ WITH GRANT OPTION ]
```

At the column level you can set the following clauses:

- SELECT: This clause allows the user to read a column

- INSERT: This clause allows the user to do some insertions into a column

- UPDATE: This clause provides the user with the ability to change the content of a column

- REFERENCES: This clause provides the user with the permission to refer a certain column

Permissions on the column level are possible and easy to implement. Especially, if you want to hide things such as credit cards, account balances, and so on; column permissions can be an important step towards database security.

Improving security with SELinux

On Linux, there is a thing called SELinux (short for "Security Enhanced Linux"). SELinux enables fine-grained access control and allows end users to define sophisticated security policies. Many users turn off SELinux simply because it is too complicated. However, it is really worth familiarizing yourself with the basic concepts to see if you can gain from implementing a policy.

If PostgreSQL has been compiled with the --with-selinux option, it is possible to integrate PostgreSQL with SELinux tightly and come up with an integrated security policy for the entire system.

The main question now is: How can PostgreSQL integrate with SELinux? The key is an instruction called SECURITY LABEL:

```
test=# \h SECURITY LABEL
Command:        SECURITY LABEL
Description: define or change a security label applied to an object
Syntax:
SECURITY LABEL [ FOR provider ] ON
{
  TABLE object_name |
  COLUMN table_name.column_name |
  AGGREGATE agg_name (agg_type [, ...] ) |
  DATABASE object_name |
  DOMAIN object_name |
  EVENT TRIGGER object_name |
  FOREIGN TABLE object_name
  FUNCTION function_name
  ( [ [ argmode ] [ argname ] argtype [, ...] ] ) |
  LARGE OBJECT large_object_oid |
  MATERIALIZED VIEW object_name |
  [ PROCEDURAL ] LANGUAGE object_name |
  ROLE object_name |
  SCHEMA object_name |
  SEQUENCE object_name |
  TABLESPACE object_name |
  TYPE object_name |
  VIEW object_name
} IS 'label'
```

As you can see, labels can be attached to pretty much every object relevant for security.

Consider the following example:

```
SECURITY LABEL FOR selinux
  ON TABLE t_test
  IS 'system_u:object_r:sepgsql_table_t:s0';
```

A security label is the mechanism used by SELinux to classify resources, such as processes and files, on a SELinux-enabled system. This context allows SELinux to enforce rules for how and by whom a given resource should be accessed.

With SELinux you can achieve a high level of security. It is a good tool for high-security systems.

Summary

In this chapter, PostgreSQL security essentials have been covered. From the instance to the column level, PostgreSQL allows you to nicely adjust your permissions and to integrate deeply into a system-wide security concept.

In the next chapter, logfiles will be covered. You will learn to configure PostgreSQL to produce the logs you need for your daily work.

4
Managing Logfiles

In this chapter, we will be covering the management of the PostgreSQL logfile. You will be guided through the most essential configuration switches. If there is anything related to administration—this is it. You will learn about various log levels and, hopefully, gain valuable insights.

By the end of this chapter, log management will be an easy task for you.

This chapter covers the following topics:

- Understanding the PostgreSQL log architecture
- Configuring log output amounts
- Making log creation more fine grained

Understanding the PostgreSQL log architecture

If you have compiled PostgreSQL from source, you will see that by default, all the logging generated simply goes to **standard error (stderr)**. Sending log output to stderr straightaway has some wonderful advantages. First of all, it scales. Every database connection produces its log independently, and therefore, there is no central bottleneck.

However, if we want to write the logging information created by PostgreSQL to logfiles, the situation will be a bit more complicated. If all open database connections would chase the same logfile to write data, there would be a serious source of contention inside the system. Dozens of database connections might wait for a single logfile. Logically, this kind of bottleneck will have a significant impact on speed—things would simply not scale.

Keep in mind that PostgreSQL has been made for high concurrency. There is no use having parallelism during execution if all processes have to wait for a single operation to complete. PostgreSQL has to scale up to as many CPUs as possible, so precautions have to be taken.

To achieve the goal of scaling log creation and writing nicely, PostgreSQL decouples log creation and log writing. Whenever a line of log is created by a database connection, it won't go to the log directly. It will be sent to a **logging collector** process instead. The logging collector process will then take care of the file's I/O. Due to this buffering, bottlenecks are avoided to a large extent and log writing can happen a lot faster.

Configuring log destinations

As we mentioned earlier, log output will end up at stderr by default. However, there are more valid log destinations you can make use of, along with stderr:

- csvlog: The CSV log
- syslog: The Unix system logging daemon
- eventlog: The Windows logging infrastructure

Creating local logfiles

Sending logs just to stderr is not too useful and won't satisfy most administrators. The goal is to provide you with proper logfiles. This is the task of the stats collector, which takes the stderr and prepares proper logfiles. Here is how it works:

```
log_destination = 'stderr'
            # Valid values are combinations of
            # stderr, csvlog, syslog, and eventlog,
            # depending on platform.  csvlog
            # requires logging_collector to be on.
logging_collector = on
```

The two settings shown in the preceding code snippet will tell PostgreSQL to write logfiles. However, which filename is PostgreSQL going to use? How large can a logfile grow and where will it reside? A set of config variables will define it exactly:

```
log_directory = 'pg_log'
log_filename = 'postgresql-%Y-%m-%d_%H%M%S.log'
```

```
log_file_mode = 0600
log_truncate_on_rotation = off
log_rotation_age = 1d
log_rotation_size = 10MB
```

In the preceding example, we want the logfile to reside in `$PGDATA/pg_log` (`$PGDATA` is the directory that contains your database instance). The name of the logfile will be defined by `log_filename`. As you can see, the name can be configured freely. In our example, the name will consist of year, month, day of the month, hour, minute, as well as seconds. PostgreSQL will use the moment of file creation inside the filename.

If you want to use different placeholders inside your filename, you can consult the man page of `strftime` to find out more:

man strftime

All placeholders supported by `strftime` are also supported by PostgreSQL.

Once we configure the filename, we can take care of filesystem permissions. In our example, we used the default value (`0600`). In most cases, this octal value is a reasonable setting. However, feel free to change things here.

Finally, it is time to control the maximum file size. In this setting, we want to make sure that a new logfile is created once a day — unless the file grows beyond 10 MB. In this case, a logfile is created when the file size is exceeded. Please keep in mind that PostgreSQL will not clean up these files. Cleanup is really an issue that has to be done by the administrator (through a cron job or so). However, there are also PostgreSQL's onboard means to rotate logfiles when there are duplicate files.

PostgreSQL will only overwrite a logfile, if (and only if) the name of the logfile is already in use and if `log_truncate_on_rotation` is on. Otherwise, the logfile will stay in place. Be careful as your disk can easily fill up if you don't take this into account.

Using syslog

Syslog is a good alternative for PostgreSQL's own log infrastructure. To configure `syslog`, all it takes is a couple of configuration switches. Here is how it works:

```
log_destination = 'syslog'
syslog_facility = 'LOCAL0'
syslog_ident = 'postgres'
```

First of all, we have to tell PostgreSQL that the log destination is `syslog`. Then, we have to tell the system which syslog infrastructure to use—we have to do this to make sure that we can properly identify PostgreSQL and distinguish it from other services on the very same server.

 Keep in mind that syslog is lousy. It means that under heavy load, messages can actually be dropped by the syslog infrastructure.

Configuring logs on Windows

Configuring a Windows system is as simple as configuring syslog. PostgreSQL offers a corresponding configuration parameter, which is in charge of telling Windows how to identify PostgreSQL.

Here is how it works:

```
# This is only relevant when logging to
# eventlog (win32):
event_source = 'PostgreSQL'
```

In our example, PostgreSQL will identify itself as PostgreSQL.

Performance considerations

During training courses, many people ask about the logging methods that offer the greatest performance benefits. The answer is basically simple: the fewer logs you produce, the faster things will be. Of course, logging is essential and, therefore, not logging is definitely not an option. So, which log destination shall someone decide on if performance is the key factor?

In general, we have found out that `syslog` is slower than the local logfiles. There seems to be some overhead in the `syslog` infrastructure, which is not present when relying on PostgreSQL internals. Of course, nothing is as fast as `stderr`, but local logfiles seem to be a good compromise here.

 If you are interested in more performance data, consider visiting our blog to find out more at `http://www.cybertec.at/logging-the-hidden-speedbrakes/`. We have also conducted some extensive performance tests.

Configuring the amount of log output

In this section, we will discuss how to control the amount of log produced by the database. The default configuration of PostgreSQL provides us only with error messages. Sometimes, this is just not enough. The goal of this section is to provide you with all the information you need to make PostgreSQL more verbose.

The central configuration variable here is `log_statements`:

```
log_statement = 'all'                # none, ddl, mod, all
```

Let's see the description of the variables used in the preceding code snippet:

- `none`: In this case, only error messages are logged (syntax errors, panics, fatal errors, and so on).
- `ddl`: At this level, we will already log all errors, including all commands that change the data structure (`CREATE TABLE`, `ALTER TABLE`, and so on).
- `mod`: In this case, in addition to errors and structural changes, we can also log statements, which change data (for example, `INSERT`, `UPDATE`, `DELETE`, and so on).
- `all`: In this case, we can finally log all statements. This includes the `SELECT` statements.

In our example, we are using a Linux system, and we want to show the effects of what we configured in the *Creating local logfiles* section, along with the change we made to `log_statements`. To activate the logging collector, we have to restart the database.

Then, we can check out the logfile, using the following code:

```
$ psql -l


  … will list all databases …


$ cd pg_log/
$ ls
postgresql-2014-06-04_161532.log
$ cat postgresql-2014-06-04_161532.log
LOG:  database system was shut down at
  2014-06-04 16:15:31 CEST
LOG:  database system is ready to accept connections
```

```
LOG:   autovacuum launcher started
LOG:   statement: SELECT d.datname as "Name",
  pg_catalog.pg_get_userbyid(d.datdba)
    as "Owner",
  pg_catalog.pg_encoding_to_char(d.encoding)
    as "Encoding",
  d.datcollate as "Collate",
  d.datctype as "Ctype",
  pg_catalog.array_to_string(d.datacl, E'\n')
    as "Access privileges"
  FROM pg_catalog.pg_database d
  ORDER BY 1;
```

As seen in the preceding code, `psql -l` will list all databases on the database server. Behind the scenes, it is just some SQL command executed by the frontend. When looking into the log directory that we defined, we will find a file that contains all the SQL executed since our restart.

> Note that if you just want to change `log_statement`, a SIGHUP (`pg_ctl … reload`) is enough. Restarting the database instance is only necessary if the logging collector is turned on.

Making logs more readable

Until now, we have managed to configure logging. However, if you take a closer look at the log, you will notice that it is not very useful yet. For instance, it does not tell us when a query was executed or who did what. Clearly, this is not enough for practical purposes. Logs are usually worthless without a timestamp. The point now is that some people need a timestamp, others are interested in users, others in process IDs, and so on. The PostgreSQL solution to the problem is that everybody will get exactly what they need. A variable called `log_line_prefix` does the job:

```
log_line_prefix = '[%t / %d / %p] - '
    #   %a = application name
    #   %u = user name
    #   %d = database name
    #   %r = remote host and port
    #   %h = remote host
```

```
#   %p = process ID
#   %t = timestamp without milliseconds
#   %m = timestamp with milliseconds
#   %i = command tag
#   %e = SQL state
#   %c = session ID
#   %l = session line number
#   %s = session start timestamp
#   %v = virtual transaction ID
#   %x = transaction ID (0 if none)
#   %q = stop here in non-session
#        processes
#   %% = '%'
# e.g. '<%u%%d> '
```

The beauty of this concept is that you can freely define the layout and content of your log. Everybody has different requirements, and therefore, PostgreSQL gives you all the power to extract exactly the kind of information you need.

Time zones are also an important thing when it comes to readability. Let's assume that you are running a dozen of PostgreSQL servers all over the world. By default, each server will write logs in its own time zone. If something goes wrong, it can be pretty painful to see whether something was wrong on all servers or not. The log_timezone variable tells PostgreSQL to write logs in a certain time zone. If you use, say, UTC on all servers, things will be easy to compare and cross check.

Here is how you can define this variable:

```
log_timezone = 'Europe/Vienna'
```

Additional settings

In addition to what you have just seen, PostgreSQL offers some more settings that you can utilize to make your log as useful as possible:

```
log_checkpoints = on
log_connections = on
log_disconnections = on
log_duration = on
```

We can log new connections (log_connections), disconnects, checkpoints, as well as, query durations. Logging the time a certain query needs is highly useful and might provide you with valuable insights into what is going on in your system. However, be careful; the log might contain something like:

```
duration: 234 ms
duration: 543 ms
```

You might see a couple of durations — but for which query? To make sure that you can figure out how long each query has taken, it makes sense to include the process ID into your log_line_prefix section. Alternatively, you can also use a session ID to do this. Those two numbers will help you unite things again.

> Note that this chapter only covers the most essential parameters that are widely used by folks around the globe. It is not meant to be a comprehensive guide.

Making log creation more fine grained

Until now, you learned how to configure logs on a per-instance basis. We changed parameters in postgresql.conf globally, and we enjoyed the fact that logging was easy and fast.

However, in some cases, we might want to be a bit more fine grained and more specific about what has to be logged and what can go unnoticed.

Logging selectively

PostgreSQL provides us with some instructions that allow us to set variables (work_mem, time_zone, logging related stuff, and so on) on a per-database basis. This can come in handy if you want to be a bit more selective. Here is how you can change logging for an entire database in your database instance:

```
test=# ALTER DATABASE test SET log_statement = 'all';
ALTER DATABASE
```

Of course, we can also do this for a user. The syntax works like this:

```
ALTER ROLE name [ IN DATABASE database_name ]
   SET configuration_parameter { TO | = }
      { value | DEFAULT }
```

The following example shows how we can make the `hs` user in the `test` database log everything:

```
test=# ALTER ROLE hs IN DATABASE test
    SET log_statement = 'all';
ALTER ROLE
```

Especially during the development phases, this can come in handy.

Focusing on slow queries

Sometimes, a DBA is only interested in slow queries. It might not be necessary to log all of them but just the really slow ones that cause performance problems. To do so, PostgreSQL provides all the necessary means. By default, the logging infrastructure does not care about the runtime of a statement; however, you can set `log_min_duration_statement` as shown here:

```
test=# SHOW log_min_duration_statement ;
 log_min_duration_statement
----------------------------
 -1
(1 row)
```

As we mentioned in the preceding code, `-1` is the default value here. It indicates that we don't want to use this functionality. However, if we change this value to, say, 1000, it means that all queries that take longer than 1 second will be sent to the log stream—regardless of `log_statement`. So, even if `log_statement` is set to `none`, we will log slow queries now. This kind of functionality can come in handy if you want to hunt down performance bottlenecks.

Silencing notices

In PostgreSQL, simple `NOTICE` messages make it to the log. Usually, this is not an issue; however, there might be cases when this floods your logs unnecessarily. Especially, stored procedures can be a source of a massive amount of logging information.

Here is an example:

```
test=# CREATE FUNCTION foo() RETURNS void AS
$$
        BEGIN
```

```
                    RAISE NOTICE 'some message';

                    RETURN;

             END;

$$ LANGUAGE 'plpgsql';
```

If we call this `foo()` function, a line of log will be issued, shown as follows:

```
test=# SELECT foo();

NOTICE:   some message

 foo

-----


(1 row)
```

If you call this function a million times, this can add up to a lot of unnecessary log information.

In the following example, we want to prevent unnecessary logging information sent to the client. In addition to this, we want to tell the log infrastructure that only messages that are at least classified as ERROR should make it to the log:

```
test=# SET client_min_messages TO 'ERROR';

SET

test=# SET log_min_messages TO 'ERROR';

SET

test=# SELECT foo();

 foo

-----


(1 row)
```

Of course, we can also use ALTER TABLE and/or ALTER ROLE to adjust things to our needs.

Summary

In this chapter, you were introduced to the basics of the PostgreSQL logging infrastructure. You are now able to configure logs in a beneficial way and reduce unnecessary log messages.

In the next chapter, you will be introduced to backup and recovery. You will learn how to dump and restore databases.

5
Backup and Recovery

In this chapter, you will learn all you need to know about backup and recovery in PostgreSQL. The following topics will be covered in this chapter:

- Importing and exporting data
- Performing simple dumps
- Creating efficient custom-format dumps
- Replaying dumps
- Scaling up replay

Importing and exporting data

Before actually diving into backup and recovery, it is useful to take a general look at importing and exporting data from, and into, PostgreSQL. Understanding imports and exports is quite essential to get the overall idea of backups on a technical level.

Using the COPY command

When talking about imports and exports, there is really no way to do it without discussing the COPY command. The COPY command is the backbone of all the operations—it makes importing and exporting to the database very easy and offers a great deal of flexibility. Here is the syntax of this wonderful command:

```
test=# \h COPY
Command:     COPY
Description: copy data between a file and a table
Syntax:
COPY table_name [ ( column_name [, ...] ) ]
    FROM { 'filename' | PROGRAM 'command' | STDIN }
```

```
      [ [ WITH ] ( option [, ...] ) ]
COPY { table_name [ ( column_name [, ...] ) ] | ( query ) }
      TO { 'filename' | PROGRAM 'command' | STDOUT }
      [ [ WITH ] ( option [, ...] ) ]

where option can be one of:

      FORMAT format_name
      OIDS [ boolean ]
      FREEZE [ boolean ]
      DELIMITER 'delimiter_character'
      NULL 'null_string'
      HEADER [ boolean ]
      QUOTE 'quote_character'
      ESCAPE 'escape_character'
      FORCE_QUOTE { ( column_name [, ...] ) | * }
      FORCE_NOT_NULL ( column_name [, ...] )
      FORCE_NULL ( column_name [, ...] )
      ENCODING 'encoding_name'
```

Basic operations of the COPY command

Basically, there are two directions here: COPY FROM and COPY TO. The first command is essential to import data. The second command is to export data to a file or to some other destination.

To test COPY, we can first create a sample data:

```
test=# CREATE TABLE t_test AS SELECT id AS a, id AS b
        FROM generate_series(1, 1000000) AS id;
SELECT 1000000
test=# SELECT * FROM t_test LIMIT 3;
 a | b
---+---
 1 | 1
 2 | 2
 3 | 3
(3 rows)
```

In our example, 1 million rows are generated. In order to export the data, the following can be done:

```
test=# COPY t_test TO '/tmp/export.txt';
```

```
COPY 1000000
test=# \q
hs@chantal:~$ head -n 2 /tmp/export.txt
1    1
2    2
```

All that has to be done is pass a filename to COPY TO. A tab-separated file will be
written onto the disk in this case.

Of course, there are countless options you can use to adjust this file as per your
needs. Some of the most common ones are CSV, along with HEADER as well as
DELIMITER ...:

```
test=# COPY t_test TO '/tmp/export.csv' CSV HEADER;
COPY 1000000
test=# \q
hs@chantal:~$ head -n 2 /tmp/export.csv
a,b
1,1
```

In this example, data is exported in the CSV format. Especially, if something has to
be prepared for Microsoft Excel or some other spreadsheet, CSV is an easy-to-use
format. It can also be quite handy to use HEADER in combination with CSV to make
PostgreSQL write the column name to the file.

If you want to import the data again, you can simply use the same line of code and
replace TO with FROM. The data will then be added to the table.

> Remember that existing data won't be replaced—the data in your text
> file will simply be appended to what is already present in the table.

There is just one catch if data has to be prepared for a spreadsheet: spreadsheets
cannot handle large amounts of data, so you have to limit the amount of data
written. The COPY query will do the job for you:

```
test=# COPY (SELECT a, b FROM t_test
        ORDER BY a, b DESC LIMIT 10000)
    TO '/tmp/export.csv' CSV HEADER;
COPY 10000
```

The result of a query can be exported just like a table. The beauty of the concept is
that you can utilize all the power of the COPY command (formats, ability to handle
delimiters, and so on) to export virtually anything.

Making use of pipes

Recent versions of PostgreSQL can tightly integrate with the operating system and support the use of pipes. The COPY ... PROGRAM command makes PostgreSQL send data to a pipe or read data from a pipe.

The goal of the following example is to import data directly from the Web:

```
test=# CREATE TABLE t_oil (    country      text,
            year        int,
            production    int);
CREATE TABLE
```

The goal here is to import production data for crude oil into our database. To demonstrate how this can be done, a file that contains some data can be found at http://www.cybertec.at/secret/oil.txt. The file contains three columns, separated by tabs. The COPY command can now be used to read the data and load it directly into the database:

```
test=# COPY t_oil FROM
    PROGRAM 'curl www.cybertec.at/secret/oil.txt';
COPY 92
```

The curl command reads the data from our web server and sends it to the pipe directly, where the data is readily picked up by PostgreSQL.

If this command succeeds, the table will contain some data:

```
test=# SELECT * FROM t_oil LIMIT 2;
 country | year | production
---------+------+------------
 USA     | 1965 |       9014
 USA     | 1966 |       9579
(2 rows)
```

The same concept can be applied to export data:

```
test=# COPY t_oil TO PROGRAM 'wc > /tmp/wc.txt';
COPY 92
test=# \q
hs@chantal:~$ cat /tmp/wc.txt
    92    322    1775
```

In this case, the data goes directly to the pipe and, therefore, to the word count. Of course, it works in both directions: writing to the pipe and reading from the pipe.

Performing backups

Now that you have seen how to import and export data in the PostgreSQL world, it is time to focus your attention on performing basic backups. The backbone of a classical, text-based backup is a program called pg_dump.

Handling pg_dump

The pg_dump is a command-line tool, easy to use, and is capable of extracting a database in a plain text format. Here is how the most simplistic backup of them all works:

```
$ pg_dump test > /tmp/dump.sql
```

The dump.sql file will contain a text representation of the database. If you happen to have data in your database, you will see that this data has been exported via COPY.

Note, pg_dump will return data as text. So, all on-board tools of your operating system are at your disposal. Here is how a dump can be compressed easily:

```
$ pg_dump test | gzip -c > /tmp/dump.sql.gz
```

> A dump can be done during normal operations. There is *no* need to shut down the database to extract a dump. Internally, a dump is simply a large transaction in the transaction isolation level named **repeatable read**. There will not be too much of an impact on the system.

In the next step, the goal is to replay the dump. To do so, a database can be created, and psql can be fired up to read in the dump:

```
$ createdb some_name
```

```
$ psql some_name < /tmp/dump.sql > /dev/null
```

For a basic backup, these handful of lines are totally sufficient.

More sophisticated dumping

Of course, this is not the end of the story. There is a lot more that pg_dump can do for you. One of the most important features here is definitely the ability to draw the so-called **custom format dumps**. What is a custom format dump? Well, it is a compressed dump, and is the important thing, including a table of contents. The point here is that you can partially restore your database if just one table, one index, or one function has gone south. One additional advantage is that restore can happen in parallel.

Here is an example:

```
pg_dump -Fc test -f /tmp/dump.fc
```

The `-Fc` variable makes `pg_dump` create a parallel dump, which can be replayed easily:

```
pg_restore -j 4 -d some_name /tmp/dump.fc
```

In this example, PostgreSQL tries to scale up the replay process to 4 CPUs. This is especially useful if many large tables are around, because PostgreSQL can then create the index in parallel. Keep in mind that creating an index can be a major bottleneck when a backup is replayed.

Performing partial replays

Before doing a partial replay, it can make a lot of sense to actually check what the backup file contains. To find this out, `pg_restore` offers the `--list` option. Here is how it works:

```
$ pg_restore --list /tmp/dump.fc
;
; Archive created at Mon Jul 14 12:15:00 2014
;       dbname: test
;       TOC Entries: 15
;       Compression: -1
;       Dump Version: 1.12-0
;       Format: CUSTOM
;       Integer: 4 bytes
;       Offset: 8 bytes
;       Dumped from database version: 9.4.1
;       Dumped by pg_dump version: 9.4.1
;
;
; Selected TOC Entries:
;
2289; 1262 16798 DATABASE - test hs
5; 2615 2200 SCHEMA - public hs
2290; 0 0 COMMENT - SCHEMA public hs
...
```

As you can see, we have a database called `test`, a schema called `public`, and so on. The `--list` variable will simply return a list of all the available objects. To partially replay the dump, you can check out `pg_restore --help` and compile the flags needed to restore the desired objects.

For example, if you want to restore a simple table, the following instruction might be of use:

```
pg_restore -t t_test /tmp/dump.fc | psql some_db
```

In the preceding command, `-t` will tell `pg_restore` which table to extract from the custom-format dump. The crux here is that `pg_restore` will simply *transform* the custom-format dump back to plain SQL, which can then be read via `psql`. Alternatively, you can also use `pg_restore` with the `-d` flag to specify the target database directly.

Passing users and passwords

Until now, it has been silently assumed that `pg_hba.conf` has some nice *trust* entries to make sure that no passwords are needed. However, in a real setup, this is rarely going to be the case. Security is an important issue, and therefore, user credentials have to be passed to the system. If a backup is created manually, you can just hammer in the password. However, what if a backup is, say, created by cron at night? There is nobody to specify the password at three o'clock in the morning.

In general, all PostgreSQL client programs provide the same set of command-line flags to define hosts, users, ports, and so on, shown as follows:

```
Connection options:
  -h, --host=HOSTNAME      database server host or
          socket directory
  -p, --port=PORT          database server port number
  -U, --username=NAME      connect as specified database
          user
  -w, --no-password        never prompt for password
  -W, --password           force password prompt (should
          happen automatically)
  --role=ROLENAME          do SET ROLE before restore
```

The important point here is that you *do not* have a command-line switch to provide PostgreSQL with a password. Why is that so? Well, just imagine somebody passing a password as a parameter—somebody else might *steal* this password by checking the process table. A simple `ps ax | grep post` command would turn into an instant security threat.

So, how to define a password then? Basically, there are two options:

- By exporting environment variables
- By creating a `.pgpass` file

Environment variables are an easy way to solve the problem. The following variables are the most widely used ones:

- PGPASSWORD: This defines a password
- PGUSER: This defines a username
- PGHOST: This defines the hostname to use
- PGPORT: This defines the port of the server
- PGDATABASE: This defines the database to connect to

There are some more environment variables around; however, for the purpose of a backup, the listed ones are enough. If you are interested in a complete list, check out the website at `http://www.postgresql.org/docs/9.4/static/libpq-envars.html`.

A second way to pass user credentials is to use a `.pgpass` file. The format of this file is simple:

```
hostname:port:database:username:password
```

Just place `.pgpass` into the home directory of the connecting user, and PostgreSQL will automatically take the credentials from there.

Dumping an entire instance

Note that until now, single tables or entire databases have been saved and restored. However, in a real-life scenario, an administrator might want to dump an entire database instance.

To do so, PostgreSQL offers a command-line tool named `pg_dumpall`. Here is how it works:

```
$ pg_dumpall > /tmp/all.sql
```

The `pg_dumpall` command-line tool will go through all databases and dump everything into a single file. In general, calling `pg_dumpall` is the easiest way to transport the entire content of a database server to some other box.

Remember that `pg_dumpall` does not provide you with the ability to create a custom format dump. It can only provide textual dumps.

To restore a dump created by `pg_dumpall`, you can again turn to `psql`. Just create an empty database instance and run the following command:

```
$ psql postgres < /tmp/all.sql
```

The system will create the databases, connect to each of them, and replay the data.

Understanding backups and user creation

When it comes to `pg_dump`, there is a small issue, which is widely forgotten by many users. When such a dump is replayed, it will create tables, set permissions, create indexes, and so on. It will *not* create the users that might be used by the system. The reason for this behavior is if you move a database from one server to some other server, it is definitely not desired to overwrite passwords on the target systems or to wildly create users who might endanger the target environment. Therefore, it is in the hands of the system administrator to make sure that all users are in place.

However, in some cases, it might be really helpful to have information about users that might have to be created. The `pg_dumpall` tool can come to the rescue here:

```
$ pg_dumpall -g
--
-- PostgreSQL database cluster dump
--

SET default_transaction_read_only = off;

SET client_encoding = 'UTF8';
SET standard_conforming_strings = on;

-- Roles
CREATE ROLE hs;
ALTER ROLE hs WITH SUPERUSER INHERIT CREATEROLE
  CREATEDB LOGIN REPLICATION;

-- PostgreSQL database cluster dump complete
```

The `-g` command tells `pg_dumpall` to extract the so-called *globals*. These globals contain user information that we might be interested in. If you dump a single database, I would generally recommend that you dump and backup these globals as well.

Summary

In this chapter, we learned how to import and export data. In addition to this, we covered backup and restore-related topics to secure your data.

In the next chapter, we will dive into the PostgreSQL transaction log. The goal is to replicate and backup PostgreSQL databases.

6
Handling Replication and Improving Performance

This chapter is dedicated to everything that is related to the PostgreSQL transaction log as well as replication. The following key topics will be covered in this chapter:

- Understanding the PostgreSQL transaction log
- Configuring checkpoints
- Setting up an asynchronous replication
- Upgrading to a synchronous replication
- Monitoring the replication

At the end of the chapter you should be able to understand, set up, and debug a typical replication scenario with ease.

Understanding the PostgreSQL transaction log

Before digging into the world of replication, it makes sense to stop for a while and focus our attention on the PostgreSQL transaction log. Many people have heard about the transaction log but surprisingly few have understood the basic principles behind this highly important data structure which is capable of making PostgreSQL as robust as it is.

The purpose of the transaction log

In theory, the purpose of the PostgreSQL transaction log or **Write Ahead Log** (**WAL**) is pretty simple. It makes sure that a database instance survives crashes. In case the power goes out or the operating system crashes for some reason, the transaction log is always there to repair the system and to save system administrators from the disaster. So, why does a database instance need a repair in case of a crash anyway?

Well, let's assume a simple example. We got a table, say, of 10 GB and we want to add a simple row, as shown in the following code:

```
INSERT INTO foo VALUES ('abcdefg');
```

PostgreSQL is going to look for a block containing enough free space to store the row. Let's assume we find a sufficiently empty block somewhere around 6 GB into the table. We grab it and start to write our row ... a, b, c ... and then the system crashes. When the system starts up again the problem is that we have an unfinished, broken row somewhere in the table. We might not even be able to locate it easily and efficiently.

The transaction log (xlog or WAL) is there to fix exactly this kind of problem. How does it work? The xlog can be seen as a tape of binary changes. Whenever changes are made, those changes are sent to the transaction log in sequential order.

> Mind that the transaction log does not contain the SQL statement — it really contains a set of binary changes. Replaying SQL would not necessarily lead to the same results. Binary changes, however, are safe and efficient.

When the system crashes, the changes can be taken and replayed to repair datafiles and so on.

But why is writing to the transaction log safer than writing to the table directly? The reason is: it is a sequential thing — the order of changes is always 100 percent clear. In addition to that, an end user will only receive a successful COMMIT message if we have made it safely into the transaction log. If the system already fails on a write to the transaction log, then the end user won't receive a COMMIT message anyway. On replay, we can see the end of the transaction log and stop after the last valid entry.

Of course, this is only a short introduction to the topic which does not span all the technical details of this area — these details are usually not relevant to administrators anyway, so I have allowed myself to skip those.

Inspecting the size of the transaction log

Once you have understood the basic purpose of the transaction log, it is time to checkout how things are actually organized on the disk.

The transaction log is (by default) stored in a directory called `pg_xlog` located in the `data` directory (`$PGDATA`). Unless it has been changed at compile time (rarely happens), PostgreSQL organizes the transaction log in 16 MB segments. These files have 24-character long filenames.

Here is an example of a pretty fresh database instance:

```
[hs@jacqueline pg_xlog]$ ls -l
total 131072
-rw------- 1 hs hs 16777216 Jul 23 13:31
   000000010000000500000075
-rw------- 1 hs hs 16777216 Jul 23 09:10
   000000010000000500000076
-rw------- 1 hs hs 16777216 Jul 23 09:10
000000010000000500000077
-rw------- 1 hs hs 16777216 Jul 23 09:10
   000000010000000500000078
-rw------- 1 hs hs 16777216 Jul 23 09:10
   000000010000000500000079
-rw------- 1 hs hs 16777216 Jul 23 09:10
   00000001000000050000007A
-rw------- 1 hs hs 16777216 Jul 23 09:10
   00000001000000050000007B
-rw------- 1 hs hs 16777216 Jul 23 09:10
   00000001000000050000007C
drwx------ 2 hs hs        6 Jul 21 19:25
   archive_status
```

The interesting thing here is the number of files around: in PostgreSQL, the number of transaction logfiles is constant. So, even if you are running a very long transaction far exceeding the size of the transaction log, the number of files won't grow.

The following are the two formulas used to calculate the size of the transaction log in PostgreSQL:

```
(2 + checkpoint_completion_target) *
checkpoint_segments + 1
```

The second formula is as follows:

```
checkpoint_segments + wal_keep_segments + 1
```

The meaning of these configuration parameters will be discussed later on in this chapter. However, it is important to understand that the way the database is used by the application does not affect the size of the xlog; however, database configuration does get affected.

How are xlog files organized? If you look into one of these files, you will see that they are basically unreadable. It is impossible to modify the xlog files.

Configuring the checkpoints

Now that you have seen what xlog is good for, it is necessary to discuss the concept of checkpoints. Let's assume we are inserting data just like we did earlier:

```
INSERT INTO foo VALUES ('abcdefg');
```

As you might expect, the ultimate goal of this INSERT statement is to write the new data to a table. In PostgreSQL, a table is always represented by a couple of datafiles consisting of 8k blocks (unless changed at compile time). The core question now is: is it desirable to write to the table directly? As discussed earlier in this chapter, writing to the table directly is not feasible anyway because in case of a crash, things would go south. Therefore, we go to the transaction log first. But this is not the end of the story as the next diagram shows:

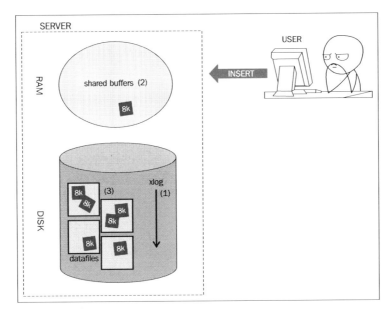

Once the data has been sent to the transaction log, a copy of the future block on disk will be placed inside PostgreSQL shared buffers—data does not necessarily have to go to the table instantly; it is perfectly fine if the data is in the xlog file and inside the shared buffers. The reason for that is simple: in case of a crash, you can always repair the table based on the xlog. The question now is whether it is desirable to write data to the data table fast or not? Well, not really. Consider somebody is repeatedly adding 1 to a certain value (maybe incrementing a counter somewhere). The very same block will be modified over and over again. If data was written to the table instantly, it would mean a modification to the table each and every time. By delaying the write to the underlying datatable, many changes might be written to the disk in just one disk I/O. The power of this optimization is incredible and it can speed up things dramatically.

Some readers might ask themselves, What if the end user ends up with wrong and outdated results in this case? The answer is no because let's assume a query comes in. PostgreSQL will check for the shared buffers first to see if there is a cached block around. The shared buffer will always have the most recent copy, so it does not matter whether the most recent blocks of an underlying table have been written to disk yet. In case of a crash, we can restore the datafiles based on the xlog anyway.

The main issue now is: we cannot write to the xlog file infinitely without ever writing to the underlying datafiles. It just is not sustainable. Remember, the xlog file is of a fixed size. The solution to the problem is a so-called **checkpoint**. The idea behind a checkpoint is to have a safe point in time making sure that the transaction log to a certain point has definitely been written to the datafiles. You can imagine that tuning the checkpoints can have a significant impact on the performance.

Optimizing the checkpoints

After this brief introduction to checkpoints, it is time to focus on optimization. To make sure PostgreSQL functions properly, a couple of parameters can be adjusted.

Configuring the distance between checkpoints

One of the most important things administrators have to tweak is the difference between two checkpoints. The further the two checkpoints are apart, the more number of options the database as well as the kernel have for speeding up their tasks (reordering, merging writes, and so on). So, distant checkpoints can speed up writes; however, there is no light without darkness. In case of a crash, all the operations since the last checkpoint have to be replayed to fix those datafiles. Logically, insanely long checkpoint distances can lead to long startup times. It can be a pretty nasty thing if your database takes a couple of minutes to start up after it had gone down because of some kernel oops or whatever.

To control the distance between two checkpoints, two variables are available, which are shown as follows:

```
checkpoint_segments = 3
checkpoint_timeout = 5min
```

The `checkpoint_segments = 3` command means that a checkpoint will kick in after 3 segments (3 * 16 MB) have been filled up. However, if the load is so low that we do not manage to fill up 3 segments in 5 minutes (`checkpoint_timeout`), a checkpoint will kick in anyway. So, the rule is: whatever happens first, `checkpoint_segments` or `checkpoint_timeout`, will trigger a checkpoint.

On a large production system, it is not uncommon to set `checkpoint_segments` to 256 and `checkpoint_timeout` to 30 minutes or so to speed up writes. However, whatever you decide on: always keep the process going on behind the scenes in mind. If there was a golden rule satisfying all needs, there would be no PostgreSQL variable to control this behavior—things would be autotuned. So, the best weapons you have are your brain and some decent understanding of what is going on here—and of course, background writer stats.

Controlling writes

Now that the distance between two checkpoints has been defined, it is important to think about what is going on between checkpoints. There are a couple of configuration parameters related to this specific question. One of the most important ones is `checkpoint_completion_target`. The general requirement is that during a checkpoint things should be written to the disk. But, in many cases, it can be wise to not write everything during the checkpoint but to gradually write data onto the disk (not all at once but step by step). The downside of writing everything during the checkpoint is that you can easily cause an I/O storm leading to lousy response times during the checkpoint. In many cases, it is way more desirable to spread the I/O load nicely.

The configuration parameter, `checkpoint_completion_target`, does exactly that. A high completion target (near 1) means that most of the I/O should already be done before the checkpoint so that not much is left. A low completion target says that data should be written out as late as possible. Writing late is ideal if you are changing a fairly small amount of data over and over again. Writing early can be beneficial during bulk loading when massive amounts of data are loaded into the database.

If you have no idea how to configure this setting, I recommend to just stick to the default value of `checkpoint_completion_target`. In many cases, this will just serve you well.

Once `checkpoint_completion_target` has been configured, we can turn our attention to the so-called "background writer". Whenever somebody makes a write (`UPDATE` or `INSERT`), data will end up in the shared buffers. This has been discussed in this chapter already. When a modification is made to block in shared buffers, the block is marked as **dirty**. In general, dirty means that the block has to be written out onto the disk at some point. Writing dirty pages out is usually done by the so-called "background writer process". Here are the parameters configuring the background writer process:

```
bgwriter_delay = 200ms
  # 10-10000ms between rounds
bgwriter_lru_maxpages = 100
  # 0-1000 max buffers written/round
bgwriter_lru_multiplier = 2.0
  # 0-10.0 multipler on buffers scanned/round
```

Basically, we have just three parameters here. Let's discuss each of them:

- `bgwriter_delay`: This parameter specifies the delay between activity rounds for the background writer. The background writer is writing in rounds and during each round a certain number of buffers are written (see the next parameter). Between these rounds, the background writer just becomes idle.
- `bgwriter_lru_maxpages`: This parameter defines the number of pages written per round.
- `bgwriter_lru_multiplier`: The number of dirty buffers written in each round is based on the number of new buffers that have been required by the server processes during recent rounds. The average recent need is multiplied by `bgwriter_lru_multiplier` to arrive at an estimate of the number of buffers that will be needed during the next round. If this is set to 1, we write exactly as many buffers as are written previously. Higher values can be used to handle I/O spikes.

Configuring the background writer is a bit tricky. It is suggested to experiment with those settings a little to see how the database behaves in your very special situation. Keep in mind that every database setup is different, and therefore, it is hard to come up with general rules. As always, a decent understanding of the underlying workings is the key to success.

Setting up an asynchronous replication

After going through the transaction log related issues, it is time to set up the asynchronous replication. The process itself is pretty simple. However, it is important to gain some overview of the problem.

Obtaining a high-level overview

So, before digging into details, I would like to list the steps necessary to set up a streaming replication slave.

 Slaves are always read-only. Writes are not allowed on slaves.

The steps are as follows:

1. Install PostgreSQL and create a `data` directory in the slave as follows:
   - `mkdir /data`   `# for example`
   - `chmod 700 /data`   `# to start PostgreSQL`
   - `chown postgres.postgres /data`   `# if running as postgres`

2. Edit `postgresql.conf` in the master:
   - Set `wal_level` to `hot_standby`
   - Set `max_wal_senders` to a reasonably high number
   - Set `hot_standby` to on (for making things easier later on)

3. Edit `pg_hba.conf` in the master and add replication rules to make sure remote boxes can connect to your server.

4. Restart PostgreSQL on the master.

5. Create an initial backup of the master on the slave. Backups can be created using `pg_basebackup`.

6. Create or modify `recovery.conf` on the slave.

7. Start the slave.

 All these steps are compiled on a single nice document which can be found at `http://www.cybertec.at/media/in-5-minuten/`.

As you can see, setting up a PostgreSQL slave is fairly easy.

Setting up replication step by step

Once you have gained some overview of the process, the first slave can already be set up. This time the process is explained in more detail. In our example, we will be using two servers. One is the master and the other is the slave.

We assume that the `data` directory of the master is `/data` and that the master is listening on `5432`.

Preparing the slave

The first thing to be done is to set up a slave. Let's assume that PostgreSQL has already been installed:

```
slave$ mkdir /data
slave$ chown postgres.postgres /data
slave$ chmod 700 data
```

The slave is now ready for further action.

Configuring the master

Once the slave has been prepared, our attention can be turned to the master. Actually, all you have to do is change a handful of parameters in `postgresql.conf`:

```
wal_level = hot_standby
```

The first thing you have to do is to teach PostgreSQL to produce enough transaction logs for replication. If we are replicating entire database instances a lot more information is needed than in the case of a simple crash. To make sure that enough transaction logs are created, the `wal_level` variable has to be adjusted, as shown in the preceding command.

In the next step, we have to tell our master that it should allow connections from the slave streaming transaction logs. The `max_wal_senders` variable limits the number of processes available on the master for this purpose:

```
max_wal_senders = 5
```

If you are planning to run just one single slave, I would still recommend setting `max_wal_senders` to at least 3 or so. During an initial backup, 2 connections can be used. So, if you have an active slave as well as an initial backup running, you are already at 3 connections. The memory footprint of a higher `max_wal_senders` setting is absolutely irrelevant—it is more of a security issue.

Actually, those two settings are already enough for a basic set up. However, later in the process, you will see that the entire configuration file is copied from the master database. To avoid going to `postgresql.conf` twice, we can already set `hot_standby` on the master knowing that the master will ignore the setting:

```
hot_standby = on
```

The `hot_standby = on` command means that the slave will be readable, and that it can be used for read-only transactions.

As far as `postgresql.conf` is concerned, this is already enough. Our attention can now be shifted towards `pg_hba.conf` which is in charge of handling the network access. Remember, to connect to a PostgreSQL server from a remote box, you will need proper `pg_hba.conf` entries.

Here is an example of a useful set of `pg_hba.conf` rules:

```
# TYPE   DATABASE      USER      ADDRESS            METHOD
host     replication   postgres  192.168.0.0/24     md5
```

The rule says: if somebody tries to fetch the transaction log from any IP in the 192.168.0.* range, a password has to be sent. The most important thing here is that the second column *must* contain `replication`. The `all` variable is not sufficient as it only means all databases.

Once these steps have been performed, the database instance can be restarted:

```
/etc/init.d/postgresql restart
```

If you don't have an `init` script, the following line will work as well:

```
pg_ctl -D /data -l /dev/null -m fast restart
```

The master has not been fully prepared for replication.

Fetching an initial backup

In the next step, an initial backup has to be created. It works like this:

```
slave$ pg_basebackup -h master.postgresql-support.de
  -D /data/ --checkpoint=fast
  --xlog-method=stream -R
```

The -h variable will tell `pg_basebackup` where to look for the master. We just have to point to our desired master. Then -D can be used to tell the system where to put the data in the target system (keep in mind that `pg_basebackup` has to be executed on the target system). The `--checkpoint=fast` command is an optional setting. Basically, `pg_basebackup` can start doing its work soon after the master checkpoint. A checkpoint will kick in on the master eventually. However, if you are testing locally, it might take some minutes to reach a checkpoint. That's somewhat nasty. To avoid this, `--checkpoint=fast` can enforce a checkpoint in the master, making sure that the data will be copied instantly.

In addition to that, there is `--xlog-method=stream`. Consider the following scenario: a large database, say 10 TB, is copied over to the slave. It takes hours to copy a database of this size, even over a fast network. During the time needed to copy our database, a lot of transaction logs might be created on the master. The master might checkpoint for dozens or hundreds of times. When the master checkpoints, it recycles transaction logs so that at the end of the long backup the xlog needed to `repair` the slave is no longer there. In short, the slave would not be able to start up without active transaction log archiving, which is covered later in this chapter.

The `--xlog-method=stream` command makes sure that a second connection is opened to the master, which is used to stream xlog while the backup is performed. This second connection makes sure that once recovery is started, there is enough xlog around to reach at least a consistent state. In other words: if you run `pg_basebackup` with `--xlog-method=stream`, you will end up with a self-sufficient backup, which can fire up easily.

Then, there is this optional -R flag. A working replication setup needs a configuration file called `recovery.conf`. It contains all the information needed to connect to the master and so on. The `pg_basebackup` variable needs virtually the same information. So, why not autogenerate the configuration? The -R variable will provide us with a simple `recovery.conf` setup so that you don't have to type the configuration yourself.

Once the base backup has been performed, all the files inside the master instance are copied over:

```
slave$ ls -l
total 116
-rw------- 1 postgres postgres      4 Aug  6 09:38
  PG_VERSION
-rw------- 1 postgres postgres    209 Aug  6 09:38
  backup_label
```

```
drwx------ 6 postgres postgres  4096 Aug  6 09:38
  base

...

-rw------- 1 postgres postgres 21231 Aug  6 09:38
  postgresql.conf
-rw-rw-r-- 1 postgres postgres   107 Aug  6 09:38
  recovery.conf
```

The base backup is now available. We are almost done.

Creating and modifying the recovery.conf file

In the next step, `recovery.conf` can be inspected. As mentioned earlier, this file has been autogenerated with the help of the `-R` flag.

Here is what the file looks like in my case:

```
slave$ cat recovery.conf
standby_mode = 'on'
primary_conninfo = 'user=postgres
  host= master.postgresql-support.de
  port=5432
  sslmode=disable
  sslcompression=1'
```

In a basic setup, there are just two central parameters. The `standby_mode=on` parameter says that replication should go on forever (until a failover or whatever). Then the connect string to the master is defined. It contains the same information that we have passed to `pg_basebackup`. It is basically the same thing.

Firing up the slave

Once the base backup is in place and once `recovery.conf` has been adjusted, the slave can be fired up (assuming that the `init` script is correct):

```
slave$: /etc/init.d/postgresql start
```

The database should be up and running now.

Note that if the slave and the master are on the same system, we need to make sure that each system has its own port.

On my system, I have the following log:

```
LOG:   database system was interrupted; last known up
  at 2014-08-06 09:38:42 CEST
LOG:   creating missing WAL directory   "pg_xlog/archive_status"
LOG:   entering standby mode
LOG:   redo starts at 5/76000028
LOG:   consistent recovery state reached at 5/760000F0
LOG:   database system is ready to accept read only connections
LOG:   started streaming WAL from primary at 5/77000000 on timeline 1
```

You should be looking for one essential line: `consistent recovery state reached`. This line is a major step to safety. If you manage to reach a consistent state, the database will be readable and you can make use of it. If you cannot reach a consistent state, something has gone south.

The slave can already be used for read-only transactions:

```
test=# SELECT 1+1;
 ?column?
----------
        2
(1 row)


test=# CREATE TABLE a (aid int);
ERROR:  cannot execute CREATE TABLE in a read-only transaction
```

Turning slaves into masters

Sometimes, it is necessary to turn a slave into a master. Especially when a master goes down, a slave might have to take over.

Promoting a slave is easy. Here is how it works:

```
slave$ pg_ctl -D /tmp/slave/ promote
```

In the previous line of code, `promote` does the job.

The following output can be observed:

```
server promoting
LOG:   received promote request
FATAL:   terminating walreceiver process due to administrator command
LOG:   record with zero length at 5/77000DE0
LOG:   redo done at 5/77000DA8
LOG:   selected new timeline ID: 2
LOG:   archive recovery complete
LOG:   database system is ready to accept connections
LOG:   autovacuum launcher started
```

The line you should be looking for is `database system is ready to accept connections`. It will tell you that your slave has successfully been promoted to a master. There is no more streaming going on.

> Keep in mind that declaring a slave to a master does not have any impact on the old master. If you have not taken down your old master, you have two masters independent of each other now. In many cases, this can be desirable—in some this is not.

Upgrading to synchronous replication

Many people are looking for synchronous replication. I have decided to include this section in this book to clear the fog and to remove some false beliefs about synchronous replication.

First of all, the goal of synchronous replication is to narrow the window of data loss in case a server crashes. Asynchronous replication means that data is replicated with a slight delay. Synchronous replication asks the slave if the data has ended up there safely. It does not exactly guarantee that no data can be lost under any circumstances. However, it makes data loss pretty unlikely.

The second thing you have to know about synchronous replication is that you should only use synchronous replication if you have *at least* three servers. Why that? Well! The idea behind synchronous replication is that your data is so valuable that you want to have it at least on two servers. But what will happen if one of those servers just dies? There is only one left and the core promise cannot be kept up anymore. PostgreSQL has a simple strategy to enforce that data has to be on two servers; it stops accepting writing transactions if there is just one box around, which is capable (allowed) of performing synchronous replication.

The third important thing has to do with performance. Keep in mind that synchronous replication can be slower than asynchronous replication because there is a lot of networking overhead around. In many cases, we are not talking about 1 or 2 percent here—we are talking about a lot more (depending on the network, of course).

Once you have decided that synchronous replication is really necessary, things can be set up. Basically, setting up synchronous replication takes just two parameters.

On the master, we need `synchronous_standby_names`. Just list the names here, for example, node1, node2, and node3.

On the slave, we have to attach an `application_name` to the connect string (`primary_conninfo`). Here is an example:

```
primary_conninfo = 'user=postgres
  host= master.postgresql-support.de
  port=5432
  application_name=node1'
```

The slave will connect to the master and pass the `application_name` variable. Then, those active slaves will be compared to the `synchronous_standby_names` variable. The first in the list will be treated as a synchronous slave (not all of them). That's somewhat important because if each slave was synchronous, the entire setup would be way too slow.

Improving and monitoring the replication

Until now, a basic replication setup has been discussed and we can work on improvements, monitoring, as well as slight extensions to the existing concepts.

Keeping an eye on streaming

The most important task of every DBA is to make sure that your setup keeps working—no matter what happens. To achieve this goal it is highly important to keep an eye on replication and to monitor things carefully.

The easiest way to monitor replication is to inspect `pg_stat_replication`:

```
test=# \d pg_stat_replication
  View "pg_catalog.pg_stat_replication"
     Column         |          Type                 |
------------------+---------------------------------
 pid                | integer                       |
```

usesysid	oid	
usename	name	
application_name	text	
client_addr	inet	
client_hostname	text	
client_port	integer	
backend_start	timestamp with time zone	
backend_xmin	xid	
state	text	
sent_location	pg_lsn	
write_location	pg_lsn	
flush_location	pg_lsn	
replay_location	pg_lsn	
sync_priority	integer	
sync_state	text	

For every slave connected to the master, a line can be found in this system view. The client_* fields will tell you where the streaming connection comes from. The backend_start field will tell you when the streaming connection was established. Then comes the state field which tells you in which state the connection is currently in.

To figure out how far your slave has progressed, there are a couple of fields available: sent_location, write_location, flush_location, and replay_location. Finally, there are two fields giving us insights into priorities.

If you don't see an entry in this system view, you might be in trouble because your slave is not connected anymore.

Making things more robust

The best monitoring in the world is in vain if the system is not robust by design. The problem with the current setup, as described in this chapter, is pretty simple. In general, the master only keeps as much transaction log as it needs to restore itself in case of a crash. Depending on the configuration of checkpoint_segments, the amount of transaction logs there can be more or less — the higher checkpoint_segments is the more xlog files you will see. The master does not care about its slave. So, if the slave falls behind for some reason (a reboot, a lousy network connection, or something similar), the slave might not be able to fetch the transaction logs anymore. A problem like that can turn your slave into a sitting duck not capable of moving forward.

To prevent this from happening, you can set a variable called `wal_keep_segments` on the master. The idea behind this is to make the master keep more transaction logs than absolutely necessary. If you set `wal_keep_segments` to `1000`, it would mean that you would have *16 MB * 1000 = 1.6 GB* of additional transaction logs around. The benefit is that the maximum downtime of the slave is then a bit more than 1.6 GB.

I highly recommend to always set `wal_keep_segments` to a reasonably high value to make sure that there is enough room for the slave to catch up. If there is enough space, I tend to go for `1000`. Why so much? Well, if you have a master and a slave, it might happen that during a bulk load the slave falls behind due to a weak network (compared to the disk speed). To prevent the slave from falling too far behind, a large value might be beneficial.

Managing conflicts

A lack of xlog is not the only thing that can harm your database system. Some users are struck by a phenomenon, which is, to at least some, pretty unexpected replication conflicts.

The core question now is, if we have a master and a read-only slave, how can we ever come up with a conflict? Consider the following scenario summed up in a little table:

Master	Slave
	`BEGIN;`
	`SELECT * FROM foo ...`
`DROP TABLE foo ...`	`...`
	`... - conflict`

As you have seen in this chapter, the slave is fully readable—a nice feature which can help you to scale out your reads nicely. But what happens if a slave starts to read a table? Let's assume it is a long read.

In the meantime, somebody drops the very same table on the master and commits. Of course the transaction log is replicated to the slave. The slave reads the xlog and figures out that the operation it is supposed to perform conflicts with the long reading transaction. What shall be done? In the most simplistic case, two configuration variables are here to control PostgreSQL's behavior:

```
max_standby_archive_delay = 30s
max_standby_streaming_delay = 30s
```

The `max_standby_archive_delay` variable says that PostgreSQL will, in case of a conflict, wait for 30 seconds before the connection on the slave causing the issue is killed. So, the solution to the problem is to remove the problematic lock on the slave by removing connections in question.

Application developers have to be highly aware of this issue because applications must be able to handle failures like that in a reliable way.

 Even without replication, application developers must be able to handle connection and query failures, and so replication should not add additional complexity to your software.

When using `max_standby_*` variables, there is something that must not be forgotten: in case of a conflict, the slave will actually wait for 30 seconds; so the slave will fall behind a little. In case of many conflicts, this can be an issue in some nasty corner cases.

The DROP TABLE command is not the only thing which can cause issues. Consider the following example:

```
DELETE FROM foo;

VACUUM foo;
```

In case DELETE is the only transaction around, VACUUM can reclaim the space shortly after DELETE has committed. Of course, those changes will be sent to the transaction logs and will be replicated. Now, what if a transaction on the slave needs the data, which is about to be removed by VACUUM? PostgreSQL will apply the same strategy, wait and kill, in case it is necessary.

However, there are other settings that can help you to fight conflicts: `vacuum_defer_cleanup_age` can be set to tell VACUUM on the master (there is no VACUUM on the slave, cleanups are coming through the transaction logs) to delay VACUUM by a certain number of transactions. In the previous example, VACUUM would cleanup things at least, say, 1000 transactions later giving the slave some time to finish its queries, which are still in need of the data.

Finally, there is `hot_standby_feedback`, which in my opinion is the best way to fight replication conflicts. The idea here is to make the slave report back its oldest transaction ID. The masters can then react accordingly and adjust its VACUUM process by delaying things as needed.

Handling point-in-time recovery

Now, let's leave replication for a while and turn our attention to backups.

Replication is widely used to secure databases and to scale out reads. A similar technique can be used for backup purposes only: **point-in-time recovery (PITR)**. In case of replication, the transaction log is replicated more or less instantly to make sure that those slaves have up-to-date data. The purpose of PITR is to replay transaction logs maybe days or weeks later to restore the database for a certain point in time.

Here is a practical example: let's assume we have done a base backup around midnight. All the transaction logs since then have been kept safely on a backup server. Now it is 5 p.m. and you have just found out that something important has been deleted at 3 p.m. What you can do now is to take your base backup, replay all the transaction logs up to 2:59 p.m. and move on from there. So, with a base backup on you can magically beam the database to a certain point in time of your choice. PITR is a wonderful feature because it removes the problem imposed by nightly textual backups. In case of a textual backup, all you can do is to restore a fixed moment in time — there is no flexibility. PITR lifts this restriction and allows you to replay exactly up to the point where things started to turn sour.

Setting up PITR

After this brief theoretical introduction to PITR, it is time to dive into the subject matter and do an actual setup.

The main steps are simple; the first thing to do is to change some parameters in `postgresql.conf`:

- `wal_level`: Set this parameter to archive or higher. I usually set it to `hot_standby` to leave the door for streaming replication open.
- `archive_mode`: Turn this parameter on to enable archiving.
- `archive_command`: This parameter tells PostgreSQL how to archive transaction logs.

Here is an example of reasonable settings:

```
wal_level = hot_standby
archive_mode = on
archive_command = 'cp %p /mnt/archive/%f'
```

In this example, the transaction log is sent to `/mnt/archive`. To keep the example simple, we just assume that `/mnt/archive` is some NFS share or so. The important thing here is that you can use any shell command or any shell script to archive the xlog. The rule is simple: if your script returns `0` as the exit code, PostgreSQL considers the command to be successful — if any other value is returned, PostgreSQL will try again after some time.

 Note that a transaction logfile is archived as soon as it has been filled up. The `%p` and `%f` fields are placeholders here. The `%p` field is the transaction logfile including the path. The `%f` field is just the filename without any path.

After changing `postgresql.conf`, the database instance has to be restarted.

 Note that changing `archive_mode` does need a restart while `archive_command` can handle `SIGHUP` (`pg_ctl reload`).

Then it is time for an initial base backup. In the previous section, you have already seen how this can be done. The very same method can be applied to base backups for PITR. However, many people prefer a second and more traditional approach. To use a simple `rsync` to backup a database instance, you first have to set PostgreSQL to the backup mode:

```
postgres=# SELECT pg_start_backup('some_name');

 pg_start_backup
-----------------
 5/78000060
(1 row)
```

The `pg_start_backup` variable waits for a checkpoint and then returns the transaction log's position. The `some_name` variable is just a label you can set for documentation purposes.

In the next step, the entire content of the `data` directory can be copied. Some prefer `rsync` to do that, however, any of the methods are fine. Here is an example:

```
rsync -rv * postgres@slave.postgresql-support.de:/data/
```

Once this command has run, the backup mode can be stopped:

```
postgres=# SELECT pg_stop_backup();

 pg_stop_backup
```

```
----------------
 5/783A0160
(1 row)
```

And voila, here is your base backup. There is nothing else to do.

> Keep in mind that during the base backup your master system can be used normally. There are no locks and no other implications (apart from some additional I/O). It is not necessary and not desirable to reduce the time window spent inside the backup mode. An active backup mode is not harmful at all.

Now, if you execute writing transactions on your system, you will see that the number of xlog files in `/mnt/archive` starts to grow.

Replaying transaction logs

The time has come: your master server has crashed and you want to recover your data until a certain point in time. Performing this kind of recovery is easy. All you have to do is:

1. Take your initial base backup.
2. Come up with a file called `recovery.conf`.
3. Define `restore_command` and tell PostgreSQL where to look for xlog.
4. Set `recovery_target_time` as you desire and tell PostgreSQL when to stop replaying xlog.
5. Start the server.

This is exactly what we are going to do. The main core question is: what might a potential `recovery.conf` file look like? Here is an example:

```
restore_command = 'cp /archive/%f %p'
recovery_target_time = '2020-01-04 12:34:45'
```

In this example, the assumption is that `/archive` has all the xlog archived by the master. We copy those files one by one to the desired location. Again, `%p` and `%f` are placeholders for the files copied.

Then, I have put an optional configuration parameter into this example: `recovery_target_time`. If `recovery_target_time` is not defined, PostgreSQL will try to recover as far as possible (until it runs out of xlog). In case a valid `recovery_target_time` is provided, PostgreSQL tries to recover exactly until the time specified.

Once `recovery.conf` is in place, PostgreSQL can be started:

```
LOG:    database system was interrupted; last known up at 2014-08-07
14:19:31 CEST
LOG:    creating missing WAL directory "pg_xlog/archive_status"
LOG:    starting point-in-time recovery to 2020-01-04 12:34:00+01
LOG:    redo starts at 5/7A000028
LOG:    consistent recovery state reached at 5/7A0000F0
LOG:    database system is ready to accept read only connections
LOG:    redo done at 5/7A0000F0
LOG:    selected new timeline ID: 2
LOG:    archive recovery complete
LOG:    database system is ready to accept connections
LOG:    autovacuum launcher started
```

The database fires up and eventually reaches a consistent state. Then it tries to reach the year 2020, which does not work, and finally becomes active.

The `recovery.conf` file is renamed to `recovery.done` to indicate that the existing database instance is the product of replication or some PITR process. The database system is fully usable now.

Of course, there are some more configuration parameters to configure the process in detail but this is beyond the scope of this book.

Understanding timelines

Until now you have seen how to set up a single slave. Basically, having more than just one slave is easy. Just repeat the process that consists of the creation of `pg_basebackup` and `recovery.conf`. This is all it takes to create more slaves on the fly. Of course you can also simply clone existing base backups.

Running many slaves in parallel is easy; however, the failover process is not too trivial. For the sake of simplicity, let's assume there is one master and two slaves. What happens if the master dies? The answer is nothing. PostgreSQL does not care. Those two slaves will try to reconnect again and again but otherwise nothing will happen—there is no automatic failover process.

Your task is to elect a new master and make sure that things can move on as expected. And this is when timelines start to matter. If you start your setup from scratch, everybody will be in timeline 1. As soon as a slave is promoted to master, it will automatically move to timeline 2. So, let's assume we have got one master and two slaves. The master dies. This leaves us with two slaves in timeline 1. One slave is promoted to master which sends it to timeline 2. We would have utterly destroyed our cluster because timelines won't match anymore. Therefore, a more sophisticated approach is needed.

If we are left with two slaves after the master crashes, the first thing to do is to figure out which slave has already received most of the data—which one is more advanced? Remember, this is an asynchronous replication. It does not guarantee that all slaves will have the same data at the same time. There is always a chance that one box is a couple of bytes ahead. So, how can we detect the position inside the transaction log to elect a new master?

Here is how it works:

```
test=# SELECT pg_current_xlog_location();
 pg_current_xlog_location
--------------------------
 5/7B0008D0
(1 row)
```

We can call `pg_current_xlog_location` on every remaining node and elect a new master. But, this is not sufficient yet. Remember, if we blindly promote a box, it will automatically move to the next timeline. So, once a new master has been chosen, all the remaining slaves must be adapted and connected to the new master in spe. How can we achieve that? We can simply change `recovery.conf` and signal the slave. It will then connect to the new server. Now the system is in a state in which there are two slaves—one connected to the other. Then, we can safely promote the desired server. It will jump to timeline 2 and replicate this change to the slave, which is not in timeline 2.

We are left with a master and a slave—just like desired. In case a second slave should be added again, normal procedures can be applied (`pg_basebackup`, `recovery.conf`, and so on).

The importance of timelines

Timelines are an important issue because they protect a database instance from imminent disaster. Why disaster? Let's assume a simple setup consisting of a master and a slave. The slave is then promoted. Remember: the slave is a binary copy of the master and so it also inherits the archive command and the rest of its features. So, if somebody happens to promote a server in a bad moment, it can happen that both servers create a transaction logfile with the same name and send it to the archive—a race condition leading to a disaster.

Timelines are here to solve the problem. Let's take a look at an xlog file:

```
00000002000000050000007C
```

The thing here is: after a string of zeroes, there is a number (in our case 2). It represents the timeline. Then comes the rest of the xlog file. So, if we jump to the next timeline the filename of the xlog will change and thus the race condition outlined earlier will be eliminated.

Summary

In this chapter, you have learned the basic replication concepts. Asynchronous replication, synchronous replication, PITR, as well as monitoring have been covered in this chapter. Of course, a short chapter like this can never contain full coverage of all replication related issues. However, the most important practical topics have been described.

In the next chapter, you will learn about monitoring PostgreSQL.

7
Monitoring PostgreSQL

In the final chapter of this book, you will learn about monitoring PostgreSQL. The goal is to give you all the tools and means to check your databases in an efficient, reliable, and easy way.

The following topics will be covered in this chapter:

- Understanding the system statistics of PostgreSQL
- Producing monitoring data for Nagios
- Using Linux cgroups

Understanding the system statistics of PostgreSQL

There are several system tables and system views to check out PostgreSQL statistics. In this chapter, the most important system views will be covered and discussed. Unfortunately, there is not enough room to cover all those views in detail. However, the most important ones are here.

More information about those system tables can be found at http://www.postgresql.org/docs/9.4/static/monitoring-stats.html.

Checking out the pg_stat_activity file

The `pg_stat_activity` file is usually the first thing a system administrator will check out in case something seems to go south. The idea behind `pg_stat_activity` is to provide the administrator with an overview of all currently open connections on the server. So, you will get one line per database connection. Here is an example of my `pg_stat_activity` view:

```
test=# \x
Expanded display (expanded) is on.
test=# SELECT * FROM pg_stat_activity;
-[ RECORD 1 ]----+--------------------------------
datid            | 16798
datname          | test
pid              | 31606
usesysid         | 10
usename          | hs
application_name | psql
client_addr      |
client_hostname  |
client_port      | -1
backend_start    | 2014-07-15 10:49:44.879941+02
xact_start       | 2014-07-15 10:49:55.211023+02
query_start      | 2014-07-15 10:49:55.211023+02
state_change     | 2014-07-15 10:49:55.211025+02
waiting          | f
state            | active
backend_xid      |
backend_xmin     | 1101
query            | SELECT * FROM pg_stat_activity;
```

The query returns exactly one line, meaning that there is just one database connection around. I am connected to a database called `test`. The operating system process serving this connection is `31606`. My user name is `hs` and I am connected using my psql command-line tool. The `client_*` columns tell me that I am connected through local Unix sockets. If I had used TCP/IP, you would be able to see the IP addresses involved here. My database connection has been started at 10:49 in the morning (backend start). My transaction (`xact_start`) and my query (`query_start`) have been started a couple of seconds later.

Then comes some important stuff: `state_change` tells me when my query has become active. If this field happens to be `idle`, it means that a query has already finished. The difference between `query_start` and `state_change` will then represent the runtime of this previous query. Sounds complicated? Here is an example:

```
backend_start    | 2014-07-15 10:54:29.536983+02
xact_start       |
query_start      | 2014-07-15 11:02:30.936953+02
state_change     | 2014-07-15 11:02:44.60962+02
waiting          | f
state            | idle
backend_xid      |
backend_xmin     |
query            | SELECT pg_sleep(100000);
```

The query has terminated. It has been active for roughly 14 seconds.

The functionality outlined here is highly important because in case of short running statements it is the only chance to see what is really going on. It is close to impossible to trap queries, which are just running for some milliseconds without understanding the blessings of `state_change`.

It is also recommended to keep an eye on the `waiting` field. If you have an unusually high number of waiting connections, it is always an indicator of trouble. Remember, waiting is the slowest form of executing queries and—if queries are waiting it means that web servers can blow up due to too many connections. It can lead to users complaining and to a vast set of other problems.

Monitoring databases

Once a DBA has gained an overview of what is currently going on in the system through `pg_stat_activity`, it can be a good idea to check out what is going on in each single database.

The system view providing information about databases is `pg_stat_database`, which is shown as follows:

```
test=# \d pg_stat_database
        View "pg_catalog.pg_stat_database"
    Column      |    Type    | Modifiers
----------------+------------------------+-----------
 datid          | oid        |
 datname        | name       |
```

```
numbackends      | integer                      |
xact_commit      | bigint                       |
xact_rollback    | bigint                       |
blks_read        | bigint                       |
blks_hit         | bigint                       |
tup_returned     | bigint                       |
tup_fetched      | bigint                       |
tup_inserted     | bigint                       |
tup_updated      | bigint                       |
tup_deleted      | bigint                       |
conflicts        | bigint                       |
temp_files       | bigint                       |
temp_bytes       | bigint                       |
deadlocks        | bigint                       |
blk_read_time    | double precision             |
blk_write_time   | double precision             |
stats_reset      | timestamp with time zone     |
```

PostgreSQL will provide you with one line per database in your database instance. I want you to focus your attention on two small fields, which can give deep insights into what is going on in a system: `xact_commit` and `xact_rollback`. Usually, there are way more commits than rollbacks. Also, the relationship between commits and rollbacks stays relatively stable over time. A typical application will always have a pretty static percentage of rollbacks. However, if this trend reverses and if all of a sudden the number of rollbacks explodes relative to those commits; there might be something nasty going on which is worth investigating. In case this happens, my suggestion is to check out PostgreSQL logs and see if there is an unusual amount of syntax error or so.

The `blks_hit` and `blks_read` variables reveal the cache hit rate. The `blks_hit` variable represents the number of blocks PostgreSQL has found in the `shared_buffers` area. The `blks_read` variable is the number of 8k blocks which has to be fetched from the operating system. Therefore, the cache hit rate is defined as:

```
cache_hit_rate = blks_hit / (blks_hit + blks_read)
```

Then, PostgreSQL will tell us how many rows it has read, written, and so on.

Then, there are two more fields giving incredible insights into the potential land of disaster: `temp_files` and `temp_bytes`. Let us assume PostgreSQL has to sort a lot of data on disk or create temporary files for some other reasons—those two fields will reveal the problem causing poor performance. Consider working on `work_mem` or `maintenance_work_mem`.

Monitoring tables

Now it is time to dig deeper and see if there is enough information about tables to detect performance bottlenecks, and so on.

One of the relevant system views here is `pg_stat_user_tables`. Among others, this system view can solve two major purposes worth pointing out in this little book:

- Detect potentially missing indexes
- Gather information about the access pattern of certain tables

The previous chapter has already outlined how to detect missing indexes with the help of `pg_stat_user_tables`. From my very personal point of view, this is the most important thing you can get out of this wonderful system table. All you have to do is study the relationships between `seq_scan`, `seq_tup_read`, and `idx_scan`, as described earlier.

The second important thing (in my judgment) is that you can get a decent overview of the access pattern of the table. Are many rows written? Updated or maybe deleted? This leads to the next important observations you can make: in case the majority of your changes are updates, `pg_stat_user_tables` can give an important hint to indicate if things such as `FILLFACTOR` are ok. In case of many updates (relative to insert or delete), reducing `FILLFACTOR` of a table might be the key to success.

Of course there is a lot of other stuff in this system view (number of `VACUUM`, and so on). It is highly recommended to take a look at this information, as well to gain a full overview of what is going on in your system.

But there is more. In some cases, you might be interested in how a table is doing on the I/O and caching front, and `pg_statio_user_tables` is exactly what you might have been looking for, as shown in the following code:

```
test=# \d pg_statio_user_tables
View "pg_catalog.pg_statio_user_tables"
     Column      |  Type  | Modifiers
-----------------+--------+-----------
 relid           | oid    |
 schemaname      | name   |
 relname         | name   |
 heap_blks_read  | bigint |
 heap_blks_hit   | bigint |
 idx_blks_read   | bigint |
 idx_blks_hit    | bigint |
```

```
toast_blks_read | bigint |
toast_blks_hit  | bigint |
tidx_blks_read  | bigint |
tidx_blks_hit   | bigint |
```

At first glance, those columns might look a little confusing. Let us look at this one in detail. The `heap_*` columns will provide us with information about the I/O behavior of the core data files. The `heap_blks_read` variable represents the number of blocks for a table requested from the operating system (disk or kernel cache). The `heap_blks_hit` variable tells us how many 8k blocks PostgreSQL could retrieve from `shared_buffers`. The `idx_*` columns tell us how the indexes (all of them) on this specific table have performed.

The Oversized Attribute Storage Technique (TOAST) is used to handle large columns and rows. Remember, PostgreSQL I/O is based on 8k blocks. What if you want to store a field containing a megabyte of data? This is where TOAST comes into play. The `toast_*` columns will tell us about the I/O behavior of this data.

The `tidx_*` columns tell us about the I/O behavior of the TOAST indexing infrastructure.

Monitoring indexes

Finally, PostgreSQL offers statistics about indexes. The two important system views here are `pg_stat_user_indexes` and `pg_statio_user_indexes`. The first view gives us information about how often a certain index is used. It is highly recommended to scan this system view once in a while to figure out which indexes are not useful anymore and thus can be dropped.

The `pg_statio_user_indexes` system view tells us about the cache hit rate of the index in question.

> All the information about index I/O is here. However, in many cases this is not where you should start looking for trouble.

Note that existing data won't be replaced—the data in your text file will simply be appended to what is already there in the table.

Checking out the information in the background writer

In this section, pg_stat_bgwriter will be presented. The idea of this view is to provide users with some insight into what is going on in the background writer front. The background writer is an important part of the entire system because it makes sure that dirty buffers are written out to the operating system. Here is the definition of the view:

```
test=# \d pg_stat_bgwriter
          View "pg_catalog.pg_stat_bgwriter"
       Column          |          Type
-----------------------+------------------------
 checkpoints_timed     | bigint
 checkpoints_req       | bigint
 checkpoint_write_time | double precision
 checkpoint_sync_time  | double precision
 buffers_checkpoint    | bigint
 buffers_clean         | bigint
 maxwritten_clean      | bigint
 buffers_backend       | bigint
 buffers_backend_fsync | bigint
 buffers_alloc         | bigint
 stats_reset           | timestamp with time zone
```

The first two columns will help administrators to figure out how checkpoints have been configured. In case there are many requested (checkpoints_req) checkpoints, it means that checkpoint_segments might be a little tight because checkpoints are initiated when the system runs out of segments before checkpoint_timeout arrives.

The checkpoint_write_time and checkpoint_sync_time variables contain information about I/O and flush times during a checkpoint. If sync times happen to be high, it is never a good sign for performance.

The buffers_checkpoint variable contains the number of buffers written during a checkpoint—buffers_clean tells us how many buffers have been written by the background writer.

The maxwritten_clean variable is the number of times the background writer stopped a cleaning scan because it had written too many buffers.

The `buffers_*` fields tell us about the I/O behavior of individual backends. In general, it is better when the background writer writes data. However, in some cases, backends might write to data files directly (especially, under very high I/O load).

The last column indicates when the statistical information has been reset.

Resetting statistics

At some point it can be useful to reset statistics. If a lot of data has accumulated already, resetting statistics can make things a lot more readable.

Here is how it works:

```
test=# SELECT pg_stat_reset();
 pg_stat_reset
---------------

(1 row)
```

However, if it is just about checking what is going on, there is a more simplistic way:

```
test=# BEGIN;
BEGIN
test=# SELECT * FROM pg_stat_xact_user_tables;
-[ RECORD 1 ]-+-------
relid         | 16854
schemaname    | public
relname       | t_test
seq_scan      | 0
seq_tup_read  | 0
idx_scan      | 0
idx_tup_fetch | 0
n_tup_ins     | 0
n_tup_upd     | 0
n_tup_del     | 0
n_tup_hot_upd | 0

test=# COMMIT;
COMMIT
```

The `pg_stat_xact_user_tables` table is perfect to figure out what is going on *without* having to reset the statistics. The important thing is that this view only contains operations made by the current transaction. As soon as you commit, all counters will start all over again from scratch. An application can easily use this mechanism to debug itself just before it commits some changes.

Integrating Nagios

Integrating PostgreSQL with the Nagios monitoring system is the goal of many system administrators. In many cases, Nagios or a Nagios-compliant solution is chosen to handle monitoring, alerting, and all that.

To integrate PostgreSQL with Nagios it makes sense to check out the Bucardo project, which offers a plugin to handle monitoring nicely. The plugin can be downloaded from the website `http://bucardo.org/wiki/Check_postgres`.

Once the module has been installed, administrators can enjoy a rich variety of checks: `http://bucardo.org/check_postgres/check_postgres.pl.html`.

Depending on your type of setup, you might want to use different modules. For example, `database_size` might be a perfectly valid check if you happen to run a large scale system growing larger and larger. It is somewhat pointless if you are serving static, historic documents to end users. So, we can only encourage system administrators to think for themselves and really try to figure out what makes sense and what does not. After all, people want useful alerts and no pointless alarms.

There are some checks, however, which might be useful all the time. Here is my personal hit list:

- **Backends**: This is the number of currently open backends.
- **Connection**: Check if a connection can be opened and if basic SQL can be executed.
- **hot_standby_delay**: This is useful if replication is at work. It can help to detect replication problems quite early on.
- **Locks**: Check for a large number of locks.
- **query_time**: This can be helpful to detect slow queries.

Of course, feel free to adjust those parameters as per your needs.

Handling Linux cgroups

Many users run PostgreSQL on Linux. In case you are running more than just PostgreSQL on your system, it can be a good idea to sandbox PostgreSQL in a Linux kernel **control group** (**cgroup**) to make sure that the operating system statistics for PostgreSQL are somewhat isolated from the rest of the system. Sandboxing also makes a lot of sense, if there is more than one PostgreSQL instance on the same box. The key benefits are:

- Data for different instances is accounted for separately
- Hardware resources can be assigned to various instances directly
- A system going nuts won't eat resources from other systems

All these benefits make cgroups an investment worthwhile.

Setting up cgroups

Before we can dig into configuring cgroups, it is necessary to make sure that all important packages are present on the system.

On Fedora, the following line is needed to enable cgroups:

```
yum install libcgroup
```

On Ubuntu or Debian, the following line will solve the problem:

```
apt-get install cgroup-bin
```

Once cgroups have been installed, it is time to configure cgroups for PostgreSQL. The idea of a working setup is pretty simple: a cgroup should be created and all processes belonging to PostgreSQL should be moved into this cgroup instantly to make sure that the kernel does all the accounting and some other tasks as well.

Once the cgroup infrastructure has been installed, it is time to configure it. The central config file is located at /etc/cgconfig.conf. Here is an example:

```
mount {
   cpuset   = /cgroup/cpuset;
   cpu      = /cgroup/cpu;
   cpuacct  = /cgroup/cpuacct;
   memory   = /cgroup/memory;
   devices  = /cgroup/devices;
```

```
  freezer   = /cgroup/freezer;
  net_cls   = /cgroup/net_cls;
  blkio     = /cgroup/blkio;
}
group pggroup {
  perm {
    admin {
      uid = root;
      gid = root;
    }
    task {
        uid = postgres;
        gid = postgres;
    }
  }
  memory {
    memory.limit_in_bytes = 4096M;
  }
  cpu {
    cpu.shares = "75";
  }
}
```

The first section defines the mount points indicating the location of these controllers. Then comes a group entry; this is basically where we got started. It has been defined that the root user can manage our group called pggroup. The group will be allowed to use up to 4096 MB of memory and we assign 75 CPU shares to the group. Of course, there are many more restrictions we can add here (I/O bandwidth, network bandwidth, and so on) — it is also possible to assign individual CPUs to a group, and so on.

As you can see, it is pretty simple to create a cgroup.

In the next step, the system administrator has to make sure that processes belonging to the postgres user are actually moved into this new group. To do so /etc/cgrules.conf can be adapted easily:

```
postgres   *     pggroup
```

All that is left now is to start these cgroup services:

```
$ service "cgconfig" start
Starting cgconfig service:                          [  OK  ]
$  service "cgred" start
Starting CGroup Rules Engine Daemon:                [  OK  ]
```

The kernel will mount a filesystem for us, which allows us to extract all the logging data from the operation system. Here is an example of how this works:

```
$ cat /cgroup/cpu/pggroup/cpu.shares
75
```

cgroups are especially important if there is more than one database instance on the very same server. The beauty is that you can make sure that one instance does not eat all the resources of the others.

Summary

In this chapter, you have been introduced to some system views provided by PostgreSQL, which can be used to monitor your system. In addition to that, some basic Nagios modules have been shown. Finally, you have seen how to isolate database instances inside the Linux kernel control groups.

In this book, you have learned all important aspects of PostgreSQL database administration and many important topics have been touched right from indexing to replication and from detecting performance bottlenecks to monitoring. The most important aspects have been discussed hoping to make your daily life with PostgreSQL as simplistic as possible.

Index

A

ALTER ROLE clause 54
ANALYZE function 24
asynchronous replication
  high-level overview, obtaining 92
  initial backup, fetching 94, 95
  master, configuring 93, 94
  recovery.conf file, creating 96
  recovery.conf file, modifying 96
  setting up 92, 93
  slave, firing up 96
  slave, preparing 93
  slaves, turning into masters 97

B

backups
  performing 79
  entire instance, dumping 82
  pg_dump, handling 79
basic operations, COPY command 76, 77
bgwriter_delay parameter 91
bgwriter_lru_maxpages parameter 91
bgwriter_lru_multiplier parameter 91
binary packages
  installing 6
B-tree index
  internal structure 24, 25
  sorted order, providing 25
btree index type 29
Bucardo project
  checklist 117
  URL 117
buffers_checkpoint variable 115

C

cert method 48
checkpoint_completion_target parameter 91
checkpoints
  configuring 88, 89
  distance, configuring 89, 90
  optimizing 89
  writes, controlling 90, 91
checkpoint_sync_time variable 115
checkpoint_write_time variable 115
column permissions
  INSERT clause 61
  managing 61
  REFERENCES clause 61
  SELECT clause 61
  UPDATE clause 61
combined index 26
COPY command
  basic operations 76
  pipes, using 78
  using 75
COPY ... PROGRAM command 78
CREATE clause 59
curl command 78
custom format dumps 79

D

data
  exporting 75
  importing 75
database-level permissions
  controlling 56

databases
  creating 14
Debian
  PostgreSQL, installing on 7

E

effective_cache_size
  adjusting 41
environment variables
  PGDATABASE 82
  PGHOST 82
  PGPASSWORD 82
  PGPORT 82
  PGUSER 82
execution plans
  about 19, 20
  B-tree indexes 24
  combined indexes 26-28
  conclusions, drawing 21
  costs, calculating 20
  indexes, creating 22
  partial indexes 28
  query performance, analyzing 23
EXPLAIN ANALYZE 24
explain command
  using 19

F

Fedora 20 8
Full-Text Search (FTS) 29

G

generate_series function 18
gin index type 29
gist index type 29
GroupAggregate 39
gss method 48

H

HashAggregate 38
huge pages 36

I

ident method 48
IF EXISTS clause 56
index types
  btree 29
  gin 29
  gist 29
  listing 29
  sp-gist 29
installation
  PostgreSQL 5
instance-level permissions
  handling 51
  roles, creating 51-53
  roles, dropping 54, 55
  roles, modifying 54, 55

L

ldap method 48
Lehman-Yao B-trees
  URL 25
Linux cgroups
  handling 118
  setting up 118-120
local logfiles
  creating 66, 67
log creation, fine-tuning
  about 72
  logging selectively 72
  notices, silencing 73, 74
  slow queries, focusing on 73
log destinations
  configuring 66
  csvlog 66
  eventlog 66
  local logfiles, creating 66, 67
  logs, configuring on Windows 68
  performance considerations 68
  syslog 66
  syslog, using 67
logging collector process 66

log output amount
  additional settings 71
  configuring 69, 70
  logs, making readable 70, 71
logs
  configuring, on Windows 68
log_timezone variable 71

M

maintenance_work_mem parameter
  improving 41
maxwritten_clean variable 115
md5 method 47
memory parameters
  adjusting 35
  huge pages, considering 36, 37
  maintenance_work_mem, improving 41
  shared buffers, optimizing 35
  work_mem parameter, tweaking 37-40
missing indexes
  detecting 29-31

N

Nagios integration 117
network authentication
  contradictions, managing 46, 47
  examples 48, 49
  managing 45, 46
  methods 47, 48
  pg_hba.conf, changing 50
  SSL, handling 49, 50
network authentication methods
  cert 48
  gss 48
  ident 48
  ldap 48
  md5 47
  pam 48
  password 47
  peer 48
  radius 48
  reject 47
  sspi 48
  trust 47

P

pages 36
pam method 48
partial indexes 28
partial replays
  performing 80
password method 47
peer method 48
pg_dump
  about 79
  custom format dumps 79
  partial replays, performing 80
  users and passwords, passing 81, 82
pg_dumpall command-line tool
  about 82
  backups 83
  user creation 83
pg_hba.conf
  about 45
  changing 50
pg_relation_size command 20
pg_start_backup variable 104
pg_stat_activity file
  about 110
  example 110, 111
pg_stat_bgwriter 115
pg_stat_database 111, 112
pg_statio_user_indexes 114
pg_stat_reset command 34
pg_stat_statement function 34
pg_stat_user_indexes 114
pg_stat_user_tables 113
pg_stat_xact_user_tables table 117
PITR
  about 103
  handling 103
  setting up 103, 104
  transaction logs, replaying 105, 106
Pluggable Authentication Module (PAM)
  about 46
  URL 46
point-in-time recovery. *See* **PITR**
PostgreSQL
  databases 13, 14
  databases, creating 14

firing up 12
index types 29
integrating, with Nagios 117
system statistics 109
URL for documentation 29
version numbers 6
PostgreSQL, compiling from source
about 8, 9
contrib packages, installing 10
database instance, creating 11, 12
working 9, 10
postgresql.conf
archive_command parameter 103
archive_mode parameter 103
wal_level parameter 103
PostgreSQL installation
about 5
binary packages, installing 6
finalizing 11
performing, on Debian 7
performing, on Red-Hat-based systems 8
performing, on Ubuntu 7
PostgreSQL version numbers 6
setup, preparing 5
PostgreSQL log architecture
about 65
log destinations, configuring 66
PostgreSQL security
about 43
column rights, managing 61
database-level permissions, controlling 56
improving, with SELinux 61-63
instance-level permissions, handling 51
network authentication, managing 45, 46
schema-level permissions 57, 58
table-level permissions, handling 59, 60
TCP, configuring 44
PostgreSQL transaction log
about 85
purpose 86
size, inspecting 87

Q

query, executing steps
executor 19
optimizer or planner 19
parser 19
rewrite system 19

R

radius method 48
Red-Hat-based systems
PostgreSQL, installing on 8
reject method 47
replication
conflicts, managing 101, 102
improving 99-101
monitoring 99, 100

S

schema-level permissions 57, 58
schemas 57
search_path variable 58
SECURITY LABEL 62
SELinux
used, for improving security 61-63
shared_buffers
about 35
optimizing 35
simple binary trees
data, preparing 18, 19
using 17
slow queries
detecting 32, 33
sp-gist index type 29
sspi method 48
standard error (stderr) 65
statistics
resetting 34
synchronous replication
upgrading to 98

syntax, CREATE ROLE
  ADMIN 53
  CONNECTION LIMIT 52
  CREATEDB | NOCREATEDB 52
  CREATEROLE | NOCREATEROLE 52
  CREATEUSER | NOCREATEUSER 52
  INHERIT | NOINHERIT 52
  IN ROLE | IN GROUP 53
  LOGIN | NOLOGIN 52
  PASSWORD 53
  REPLICATION | NOREPLICATION 52
  ROLE 53
  SUPERUSER | NOSUPERUSER 52
  SYSID 53
  USER 53
  VALID UNTIL 53
syslog
  about 67
  using 67
system statistics, PostgreSQL
  about 109
  databases, monitoring 111, 112
  indexes, monitoring 114
  pg_stat_activity file 110, 111
  pg_stat_bgwriter 115
  resetting 116, 117
  tables, monitoring 113

T

table-level permissions
  DELETE 60
  handling 59, 60
  INSERT 60
  REFERENCES 60
  SELECT 60
  TRIGGER 60
  TRUNCATE 60
  UPDATE 60
TCP
  configuring 44

The Oversized Attribute Storage
  Technique (TOAST) 114
timelines
  about 106, 107
  benefits 108
transaction log. *See* **PostgreSQL**
  transaction log
trust method 47

U

Ubuntu
  PostgreSQL, installing on 7
USAGE clause 59
users and passwords
  passing 81

W

work_mem parameter
  about 37
  tweaking 37-40
Write Ahead Log (WAL) 86

Thank you for buying
PostgreSQL Administration Essentials

About Packt Publishing

Packt, pronounced 'packed', published its first book "*Mastering phpMyAdmin for Effective MySQL Management*" in April 2004 and subsequently continued to specialize in publishing highly focused books on specific technologies and solutions.

Our books and publications share the experiences of your fellow IT professionals in adapting and customizing today's systems, applications, and frameworks. Our solution based books give you the knowledge and power to customize the software and technologies you're using to get the job done. Packt books are more specific and less general than the IT books you have seen in the past. Our unique business model allows us to bring you more focused information, giving you more of what you need to know, and less of what you don't.

Packt is a modern, yet unique publishing company, which focuses on producing quality, cutting-edge books for communities of developers, administrators, and newbies alike. For more information, please visit our website: www.packtpub.com.

About Packt Open Source

In 2010, Packt launched two new brands, Packt Open Source and Packt Enterprise, in order to continue its focus on specialization. This book is part of the Packt Open Source brand, home to books published on software built around Open Source licenses, and offering information to anybody from advanced developers to budding web designers. The Open Source brand also runs Packt's Open Source Royalty Scheme, by which Packt gives a royalty to each Open Source project about whose software a book is sold.

Writing for Packt

We welcome all inquiries from people who are interested in authoring. Book proposals should be sent to author@packtpub.com. If your book idea is still at an early stage and you would like to discuss it first before writing a formal book proposal, contact us; one of our commissioning editors will get in touch with you.

We're not just looking for published authors; if you have strong technical skills but no writing experience, our experienced editors can help you develop a writing career, or simply get some additional reward for your expertise.

PostgreSQL 9 High Availability Cookbook

ISBN: 978-1-84951-696-9   Paperback: 398 pages

Over 100 recipes to design and implement a highly available server with the advanced features of PostgreSQL

1. Create a PostgreSQL cluster that stays online even when disaster strikes.

2. Avoid costly downtime and data loss that can ruin your business.

3. Perform data replication and monitor your data with hands-on industry-driven recipes and detailed step-by-step explanations.

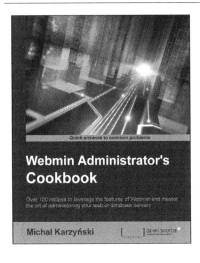

Webmin Administrator's Cookbook

ISBN: 978-1-84951-584-9   Paperback: 376 pages

Over 100 recipes to leverage the features of Webmin and master the art of administering your web or database servers

1. Configure an Apache web server, MySQL or PostgreSQL database and a Postfix mail server with the help of Webmin.

2. Install and get to know Webmin—the friendly web-based administrator's toolbox.

3. Learn how to host web applications and databases.

Please check **www.PacktPub.com** for information on our titles

PostgreSQL Replication

ISBN: 978-1-84951-672-3   Paperback: 250 pages

Understand basic replication concepts and efficiently
replicate PostgreSQL using high-end techniques
to protect your data and run your server
without interruptions

1. Explains the new replication features
   introduced in PostgreSQL 9.

2. Contains easy-to-understand explanations
   and lots of screenshots that simplify an
   advanced topic like replication.

3. Teaches PostgreSQL administrators how
   to maintain consistency between redundant
   resources and to improve reliability,
   fault-tolerance, and accessibility.

PostgreSQL Server Programming

ISBN: 978-1-84951-698-3   Paperback: 264 pages

Extend PostgreSQL and integrate the database layer
into your development framework

1. Understand the extension framework of
   PostgreSQL, and leverage it in ways that
   you haven't even invented yet.

2. Write functions, create your own data types,
   all in your favorite programming language.

3. A step-by-step tutorial with plenty of tips and
   tricks to kick-start server programming.

Please check **www.PacktPub.com** for information on our titles

Printed in Great Britain
by Amazon